D1565467

Keepin' On, Walkin' On

Keepin' On, Walkin' On

Keepin' On, Walkin' On

Keepin' On, Walkin' On
Following a Dream

by

Aleen Steinberg

Keepin' On, Walkin' On

ISBN-13:978-1979631402
ISBN-10: 1979631409

Published by The Creative Short Book Writers Project
Wayne Drumheller, Founder & Editor
Distribution USA: amazon.com

For Bill

Keepin' On, Walkin' On

CONTENTS

PROLOGUE

Prologue

I can still see my fifth grade teacher, Miss Kretschman, back in a small town in rural Wisconsin, standing in front of the room at the world map that pulled down from the ceiling, pointing out a faraway land called Nepal. I sat at a wooden desk by a window that I loved to look out of while dreaming my dreams.

Sitting at that old wooden desk, the kind with a hinged top and an ink well, and surrounded by the everyday humdrum subjects of arithmetic, reading, and writing, my world took on a new dimension as the teacher and the map introduced the country of Nepal.

Then, after reading about it in my geography book, my imagination soared and suddenly I stood amid the snowy peaks of the mysterious Himalayas. Yaks, Sherpas, yetis, forbidding peaks and fertile valleys -- someday, I told myself, I would go and see them for myself. Over the next forty-five years I dreamed of fulfilling that childhood fantasy, only to have those dreams crash when handed a chilling medical diagnosis.

Despite, or perhaps because of this diagnosis, I determined to overcome my limitations, and in the years that followed, I not only scaled the Himalayas but spent twenty years of adventure travel – climbing mountains and rafting rivers on six continents. In the pursuit of my childhood dream, I discovered not only personal fulfillment, but the shared humanity that binds us.

Keepin' On, Walkin' On

Chapter 1

Nepal

KEEPIN' ON, WALKIN' ON

Somewhere in Nepal, long before daybreak on a mountainside west of Pokhara, I awoke with a start, my heart racing from a combination of altitude and an adrenaline rush. In the darkness, my mind struggled to sort out where I was and what I was doing. The air was cool, but I felt myself cocooned in the warmth of a down sleeping bag. I could smell the canvas sides of the tent and felt the hard earth of a mountain side beneath me.

Slowly I came to terms with my surroundings. and the promise of adventure before me. Slowly I let myself believe the reality of what my body was telling me.

It was really true. I was in Nepal.

I had been a ten-year-old, sitting in a fifth grade geography class in a small Wisconsin town, when I first heard about the remote and mysterious Himalayas that would capture my imagination. For the next forty-five years I read and re-read the fantasy novel *Lost Horizons*. I researched Shangri La, Mount Everest, and Sir Edmund Hillary. I tracked down stories of the nineteenth century Gurkha soldiers whose skill and derring-do mesmerized me as much as tales of the fabled land. I devoured information about Tenzing Norgay and other Sherpas known as the *Tigers of the Snow*.

1

To scale those mountains, to walk and live among the people was the ultimate adventure and now it had begun. Although not the high adventure I'd once dreamed of, I was at last among the mountains and in their shadows to simply trek Nepal in the springtime, the season of spectacular bloom in the rhododendron forests and alpine meadows. Now I lay in my dark tent, stretching tentatively, I tested muscles, joints and ligaments for pain and stiffness and sang a quiet Hallelujah; they were in working order and could be called on to get up and go.

I had survived day one.

Those moving parts had been hard tested the day before---day one of a three week trek. We'd begun what the travel company described as an "easy half day" on the trail: an arduous 2,500 ft. climb up a steep, rocky hillside, in dusty, blazing heat past ornery water buffalo (we'd been warned to give a wide berth) followed by an hour or so of slipping and sliding in a lashing rain storm. As we trudged on, it seemed as if the gods were determined to test our mettle. They took possession of the mountainside, unleashing hail, then thunder and lightning while we huddled under the overhang of a small hut. We halted mid-afternoon to make camp. No sooner were the tents up and secured, than another storm blew through with a ferocity that was magnified by the incessant hard slapping of the canvas tent walls.

An easy half day indeed!

It might still have been just a dream, if it hadn't been for the chilling medical diagnosis handed me a year before. Fifty five, bouncing along in life with few if any health cares, my medication consisted of a one a day vitamin, period. That was before I received the doctor's report of a bone density scan. "Osteoporosis and osteoarthritis," he had said. "Prognosis not good for your skeletal type." I reeled at his words. Immediately an image popped into my mind: a close friend of mine: a tall, statuesque Norwegian woman who'd been one of Bergdorf's top fashion models, now hunched over a cane, shuffling along with the tag "Osteoporosis" pinned to her as she inched toward life in a wheel chair.

Now, that will be me, I thought. A lifetime of running, hiking, canoeing, kayaking, tennis, over, finis. I would quickly shrivel and crumple into a fragile collection of brittle bones. I could see nothing but a black void ahead. I gave in to unfathomable sorrow, put my head down and cried.

The doctor stood by perplexed, assuring me that it was not a death sentence. "But it is to me," I told him.

His eyebrows shot up. "Why?"

"There are so many things I've wanted to do, and now I won't be able to." I tried explaining as the thoughts of dreams I'd harbored for a lifetime came crashing down.

"Like what?" he asked.

"Like climbing the Himalayas," I blurted out

He was quiet for a moment, processing this personal revelation he probably didn't hear every day, maybe trying to determine if I was delusional. "Well, you'd better get started," he said matter-of-factly. "There is a new medication that promises help in some cases and I'll get you lined up with a physical therapist for evaluation. You'd better start working hard with what you have left."

He did and I did. Every day for over a year, I began my day with forty five minutes of calisthenics followed by a four mile walk at top speed. Rain or shine, in the city, in the country, on the beach or in the mountains, I allowed myself no deviation. I persevered and prevailed. With medications, and closely following the therapist's instructions, my boots were broken in and I was on my way.

As I lay in my tent, a bit of grey light began to streak through the cracks, breaking up the darkness. A Sherpa's cheerful "Good morning, Madam," sang outside my tent. "Coffee or tea?" I opened the tent flap, answered "tea, please," shook off my nighttime thoughts and looked at the new day. There before me was the world of Nepal, bigger than dreams and more magnificent than I dared remember from the day before; each peak magnified with the crystal clarity that so often follows a storm.

My dreams had ill prepared me for the range of emotions that filled me as I came to terms with the clarity of the personal storm that I'd experienced in that Doctor's office. It was difficult to catch my breath, but I didn't blame the altitude.

As I crawled out of the tent, my eyes ran over the busy camp scene. In those moments shortly after dawn, the crew was already into the well-choreographed movements of what I came to regard as the early morning dance. Mingma, the head Sherpa or *Sidar*, was overseeing the retinue that accompanied us--two other Sherpas, a cook and his helpers, and nine porters. Among them were a mother and her fifteen year old daughter who managed to carry their heavy loads while walking barefoot, even as we passed through fields of snow.

Our morning instructions were to pack our duffle bags, leave them outside the tent as a sign we were ready, take our backpack and then head to the mess tent for breakfast. We were permitted to bring thirty-three pounds of gear in our bags. The porters bound two of those bags together, secured them with a trump-line across their foreheads, loaded the sixty-six pounds on their backs and posted out.

Dressed for the day in layers of polypropylene, cotton shirt and pants, wool sweater, socks and heavy boots, I joined the group for breakfast. I took a quick glimpse around to see if any of my companions were among the walking wounded and decided all survived the first climb with no visible problems. We ate a breakfast of thick barley porridge, biscuits, strong hot tea, and were on the trail at 7:30.

We were a Duke's mixture---a strange assortment of types who had met for the first time just three days ago in Katmandu. Our group of five included an attorney given to wearing red socks and a red hat with colorful ribbons that floated down his back like a kite's tail, an architect with a surprisingly strong interest in Nepalese bathhouse construction, a dour and taciturn chemist who kept quietly to himself, a medical doctor who worked with the Apache and Navajo in the southwest. Domestic engineer was the title I gave myself. We were all accomplished hikers, but first time trekkers.

Ian, our guide, was a young Canadian who'd lived in Nepal for ten years. During our first two days in Katmandu, while our bodies had acclimatized to the altitude, he'd given us a short education on the land, its people and customs. He also gave us practical pointers to keep in mind if we wanted to finish the trek on our own two feet. Liquid consumption was one of the most important topics. "You absolutely must drink three cups of water or tea at each meal plus a quart or more during the day," he said without a trace of smile on his normally smiling face. When I heard those words I had a vision of floating down the trail but soon realized that in the high altitude of the Himalayas, it doesn't take long to become dehydrated and get sick. Or die.

Our trek was supposed to follow a main trail, but halfway through the second day Ian surprised us.

"We can stay on the designated route," he said, as we grouped around him, trying to slow our rapid breathing. "Or, if you're up to it, we can take the back ways. It might be a little more difficult, but we'd be completely isolated from other western trekkers."

I believe we were all remembering our easy Day One..

He looked around at our faces. "It could be a little risky," he said soberly. "And there's absolutely no telling what we'll run into."

As if we were one, each of us nodded in the affirmative.

I could hardly believe my good fortune. It would be an adventure.

As we left the main pathway, we entered a world that seemed suspended in time. We saw no roads----only trails worn smooth and clear from centuries of use.

The countryside we trekked those first few days covered diverse landscapes. Through pine forests, down

mountainsides of scree to a river simmering milky blue with limestone deposits, then over a swinging bridge to an area reminiscent of Florida, with citrus trees and bougainvillea in bloom.

We entered villages that hadn't seen a stranger in over a year, villages of the proud Chhetri and the scholarly Brahmans, with their houses of distinctive architecture and color. Here and there were homes of Gurkha soldiers, those fierce Nepalese soldiers that distinguished themselves fighting with the British in the Indian Rebellion of 1857. Gurkha units were closely associated with the *khukuri*, a formidable, forward-curving Nepalese knife. These knives were handsome, handcrafted, pieces of primitive art; before we left the countryside, each of us had one in our duffels.

From the heights we climbed, the terraces of spring crops looked like giant lily pads that had been halved and layered up and down the sides of the mountain. Most houses had small garden patches of greens growing beside them, little shoots of onion tops peeking up among plants resembling spinach or mustard. Here and there fruit trees were in bloom, some were citrus much like the trees that grew in my Tampa garden. As we climbed higher from the lower regions, we saw evidence of apple trees introduced by Peace Corp workers, our 20th century Appleseed Johnnies.

Sheep herder's huts, made of tightly intertwined rough branches were dotted here and there in the meadows, but no animals or men were around. The herders had taken their charges to lower pastures green with new spring grass.

Following a rocky ridge trail, we passed hillsides of barley and millet. Women and children offered welcoming smiles as they collected dried water buffalo dung to be used for their fires. Ian explained that because of de-forestation, firewood was non-existent, thus the need to fuel with these patties of dung. Carefully placed in large *dokos*, or head baskets, this fuel source was carried to a terrace where they were arranged in concise patterns to dry and harden on the rock walls surrounding the small terraces. Those terraces were so narrow, the water buffalo pulling the primitive wooden plows could barely turn around at the end of the rough furrow. These massive animals made frequent appearances the first few days of the trek; we'd give them a wide berth by stepping off the footpath, once even climbing a low rock wall as a small herd of them lumbered by.

The snowfields of the mountainside gave way to this naturalist's wonder. Fields carpeted with wildflowers and ferns, the air heavy with the fragrance of honeysuckle. We walked by trees with new leaves that looked like cut pink velvet, and bushes covered with blooms similar to yellow, crinkly sweet peas. Jack-in-the-pulpits and violets peeped out from the carpet of last year's leaves. Small birds flitted among the branches, chirping and warbling their springtime melodies.

Days later our boots found themselves in a forest of rhododendron trees, sixty to eighty feet tall, some as large as four feet at the base. Drifts of crimson, purple, magenta, violet, and pink covered the mountains-a landscape radiant with color stretching as far as the eye could see. We entered a jungle of bamboo and huge ferns, jasmine and towering dead trees whose branches held yellow and white orchids.

We passed schools where the kids ran out to greet us waving old timey primers, pointing to words and reading,

"See Dick, see Jane, run Spot run." And we laughed and shared some of our trail mix with them, smiling as they picked out the M&Ms, then finding delight as they let the little candies slowly melt in their mouths.

At times the climb seemed an almost impossible undertaking, and I had to remind myself to keep on . . . walking on. The air was thin, our route straight up, one foot in front of the other, hour after hour. We passed a salt train coming up the mountain from Tibet, donkeys plodding along with colorful plumes on their heads, heavy packs on their backs. That precious cargo was still seven days from their destination; they were getting there just like I was, one hoof in front of the other.

After a cloudy, cold day, using switchbacks to climb slopes that seemed to be forty-five to fifty degree angles we reached 9,000 feet, halted, and pitched camp in a large snowy meadow beneath forested hills. It was a blessed respite: a camp that offered an opportunity for a snowball fight, and a chance for us to fly the kites, complete with brightly colored tail ribbons, that one of the trekkers had packed along. The Sherpas laughed like kids as they ran with the kites, urging them upwards. Then with the rainbow colored tails floating beneath them, we cheered as the kites took off and soared over our heads, up, up, up, dipping and swaying high in the heavens. When the breeze stilled, the men whistled for the wind to come back and the breezes heard them.

On another gray, overcast day, after hiking in the crisp thin air had drawn on our reserves, our leader decided to pitch camp in a large meadow near a Gurung village. A serendipitous choice, for within moments villagers appeared and invited us to a dance that evening. Suddenly all thoughts of crawling into a sleeping bag right after dinner disappeared.

Later, as we arrived at a field outside the village for the ceremony, elegant leis of crimson rhododendron were placed around our necks by our new friends, a smiling, handsome people who are known in that part of the world for their rich tradition of music and dance.

On a small rise beside a glowing campfire, we hunkered down in a semicircle with the villagers, huddling in our down jackets, wool caps pulled over our ears in the chill air, as close to each other as "new-found-friend" propriety allowed.

Drums began to beat, flute music joined with a tambourine, and the dancing began. Their dances slowly depicted the events of daily life, fetching of water, of planting and harvesting crops, of flour milling, and then a surprisingly fast dance that resembled those of the free-stepping wild Kazakhs of Russia.

Toward the end of the evening we were treated to a tea ceremony, followed by a dance that was translated with the beautiful "please sit down and tell me about things you remember." This was a memory dance, weaving a story like threads laced through a loom. Dipping and swaying, joining hands for moments, then unclasping them, their bodies told the stories they lived--or the stories they had been told by those who came before them.

And we understood those stories with the humanity that binds our cultures together.

Most of our final day trekking was spent in silence, there beneath the quiet majesty of the Himalayas, as we inched our way down a precipitous mountain trail, holding on to roots and rocks for support. It was coming to a close, that trek we'd begun nine days ago, the trip I'd dreamed of, hoped and worked for, had become a reality and would find continued life as pages in a journal.

At the bottom of the 2,000 foot descent, we reached our overnight destination, a lakeside lodge that offered hot showers and beds with legs, something I'd always taken for granted, now pure bliss after being at one with the earth for nine nights.

After our farewell dinner, Mingma, the Head Sherpa who had guided and watched over us as we climbed, slid, crawled, and persevered through the challenges of our trek, presented each of us with a soft, white scarf, saying it was "something to remember us by." Draped in my sun room, the scarf, holding memories of a Nepalese walk and a Sherpa named Mingma, are part of my life today.

TRISHULI FLOAT & TIGER TOPS

Next morning we boarded a bus that took us through meadows of blue ageratum to a rocky beach where rafts awaited us. I had been sold on this trip after reading the tour company's trip description that included the lines "an exotic three day raft trip, two days at Tiger Tops Lodge with safaris in search of the Bengal tiger and the endangered Indian Rhino." Doing a tango two-step between the bus, stones and shoreline, we packed our belongings in black rubber waterproof sacks and ammo cans. Then we settled down in our rafts to begin our float on the Trishuli, a rather languid river, boasting rapids in the number two and

three category. After having rafted the Colorado and
Frazier Rivers that claim classes four and five, these rapids
seemed unchallenging. Waves maybe three to four feet tall,
a couple narrow passages between large boulders that
called for moderate maneuvering, led to unjustified
excitement when an oar was lost.

We sat back, floated and relaxed, letting our thoughts
drift by like the river's edge.. We searched the shoreline for
langur monkeys with no success. We finally sighted
Eurasian vultures, one of the world's largest birds of prey
soaring above us, with wingspans ranging eight to ten feet.
Our guide pointed out a few Brahmani Ducks paddling in a
cove, perhaps resting on their flight from India to a
Siberian summer nesting ground. Resplendent in their
monochromatic plumage of creamy white, brown, and
orangish feathers, they looked like gems of topaz catching
sunlight as they bobbed up and down in the current.

I was ready to leave the river when the trip ended.
There had been enough laid back days, leisurely dinners
around bonfires on the beach at night, enough time to rest
and reflect. It was time to move on!

At the confluence of the Kali Gandaki and the Trishuli,
we pulled our rafts to shore. Our river adventure behind us,
we boarded a bus bound for Tiger Tops in Southern
Nepal's Chitwan National Forest. Our final destination in
this country noted for its high mountain ranges, was a flat
plain known as the Terai which lay close to India, habitat of
the Bengal tigers. Maybe, if we were lucky, the tempting
lines in the trip description about sighting one in the jungle
would come true . . . and if luck was with us, we'd get a

glimpse of one-horned Asian rhinos, who also called this tall, grassy plain home.

After a bus ride that seemed interminable in the stifling heat, we finally pulled into a small clearing and transferred to a Land Rover for a short ride to a grassy field where elephants awaited us. Small ladders allowed us to reach the wooden platforms, or *howdahs*, on the elephants backs, while the elephant lifted his driver, or mahout ,with his trunk and placed him atop its head in the driver's seat. As soon our bags were loaded we were off to the promised land of hot showers and beds with fresh linen.

Our guide had given us a brief introduction to the ride, and explained how the mahout controlled the elephant. While the elephants understood a few voice commands, they were also guided by a tap on their skull with an iron rod. We wove our way through tall, dense "elephant grass" and forest, reaching the lodge built in the traditional longhouse architectural style of Tharu, the indigenous people of the Terai. The thatched lodge was built on high poles--our rooms had bamboo walls, kerosene lamps hanging on the wall and room to stand up. It was pure bliss remembering twelve days in a cramped tent.

I hurried to shower and join the group in the dining room for dinner and a slide show by Charles McDougall, author of *The Face of the Tiger,* who was conducting a study on the area's tigers. He had logged several thousand hours observing-tracking those powerful predators. His book captured and explained their life and lucky us: he was here in the area to lecture!

We were about to finish dinner and move on to the bar, when a mahout walked quickly to McDougall's table, spoke softly to him, then turned and left. "A tiger had been sighted!" We were out of our chairs in an instant, hurriedly off to the jungle to try our luck at sighting the animal. We had been given our instructions. "Follow McDougall on the packed dirt path in single file, stay close, no talking." We were to leave our shoes at the trailside when we neared the lair that had been baited with a buffalo or goat.

We moved off together in the darkness. McDougall had a flashlight with a tiny beam that he kept pointed to the ground as he led the way. My heart thumped as my eyes adjusted to the night, trying hard to see. I could only feel the presence of the person ahead of me as we walked through the darkness toward a bamboo wall that stood above a small clearing. We could hear the tiger chewing and crunching bone, and we stood like statues waiting. A pair of hands gripped my shoulders and led me to a small eye-level opening in the wall. Suddenly a dim light was turned on and there before us, a good ways distant, was maybe six hundred pounds of a Bengal tiger, slowly chewing on a water buffalo it had ripped apart.

Breathing slowly and quietly, we stared at the powerful animal who seemed to ignore the light that had suddenly appeared in his world of night, or in what might be lurking behind that flimsy bamboo wall. The tiger continued to relish the fresh meat held in his massive paws, chewing slowly, deliberately, as we stood motionless staring into the night before us.

Moments passed, then I shared the soft "Let's go" tap on my shoulder to the person next to me, and slowly, silently we filed out of the blind, back to the path. Picking up our shoes, we padded back to a clearing, re-shoed, then returned to the Lodge. I was lost in thoughts of William Blake's poem *The Tyger*, one I'd had to memorize back in an eighth grade classroom, words that had burned a fearful orange and black image in my brain. Now I'd come face to face with it. The tiger could be watching me, and wondering about the stars and fire in my eyes.

Our itinerary offered a couple days at Tiger Tops, with activity centered mostly around taking it easy after the rigorous trek, and spending time with elephants. The elephant yard held ten to fifteen elephants, all chained or tethered, and with our experienced naturalist and guide, we were encouraged to walk up to them, speaking softly, offering our hand for a trunk kiss, and even giving them a head bump. After a few moments in the presence of a swaying gray mound of massive muscles and wrinkled skin, one elephant extended its trunk toward me, examining my arms and face, touching them ever so gently with little butterfly-like strokes and kisses. And then, looking into the eyes of that animal I experienced another never-to-be-forgotten moment. Its eyes seemed to say, "Yes, I'm chained to this life." I wanted to cut its leg irons and yell "Go, run free."

When the elephants were brought to a special loading platform off the side of a building, we climbed a ladder and settled ourselves into the *howdah.* Old stuff the second time around. This morning we were off to the jungle in search of the one-horned rhino, and maybe, just maybe, catch a glimpse of a tiger among the tall trees or the open spaces covered with ten foot tall elephant grass. Silence was again the order of the day, as we left the clearing.

We moved through the forest quietly and out onto a savannah, then along a river bank covered with yellowish, feathery elephant grass. As we swayed atop the huge animals, the only sounds we heard were the soft plod of the elephant's feet and an occasional bird song. We spotted a langur monkey swinging through the trees, its maneuvers the envy of any Ringling aerialist, as it swung from branch to branch, pausing every now and then to look at the circus below, then gliding out of sight.

Mid-morning our safari slowed, the lead Mahout held up his arm and pointed toward a huge, soft, milky gray mound in the grass, and there it was, a one horned Rhinoceros, with a baby close by its side. The mother turned to stare at us, about two ton of armor-plated life, maybe six feet tall, her small eyes set beneath big mitten-like ears. From my perch atop the elephant, the rhino appeared smaller than I expected, but the power of those couple tons of life was palpable across the space between us.

Then turning, she ambled off into the bush, with baby close beside her. Our oath of silence was broken by the clicks of cameras.

Back at the elephant compound, we'd just dismounted when the sound of an elephant trumpeting and the pounding of its hooves charging toward us reached our ears. We stood in dumb amazement as an elephant, with a wild eyed, grim faced mahout atop it, urged the animal on while a frenzied woman in the *howdah* wielded an umbrella about and upon his shoulder. When the elephant thundered to a stop at the loading platform, the woman crawled out still shouting.

Slowly the story unfolded. The woman had taken exception to the driver's use of the steel rod to direct the elephant by hitting it on its head. She decided that "turnabout was fair play," took her umbrella and began striking the man's shoulder. "Again and again," he reported, while two others along on the ride nodded their heads and verified his story, as the woman stomped to the cocktail lounge.

On the morning of departure, our trek finished, our bags packed, our jeep ready to carry us to the landing strip-we suddenly became aware of a medical emergency in our group.

Seems the night before, our architect/trekker companion, interested in the construction of the bamboo bath houses, had ventured into a no-man's land behind the building and stepped into a septic tank, falling in waist deep. Rescued, hosed down repeatedly, bathed repeatedly, he'd spent a sleepless night and now shook with chills and fever. The doctor in our group speculated that he'd most likely contacted Giardia. Medical books tell us that Giardiasis is an illness caused by a parasite called *Giardia intestinalis*. It lives in soil, food, and water. It may also be on surfaces that have been contaminated with waste. You can become infected if you swallow the parasite. You can also get it if you're exposed to human feces (poop). Well, it figured.

The ride to the field where our plane waited was a quiet one, each of us lost in thought. I struggled to imagine what the man had experienced before he was rescued, and wondered if anyone would ever believe his story. We arrived at the plane. Two rear seats had been removed, a stretcher brought in. The patient was belted in and we were off to Kathmandu, to medical attention. and then a plane that would take us back home.

A Nepalese doctor awaited us at the hotel; we watched as our companion was wheeled to his room, our fellow MD accompanying them. We were grateful this professional was there to assist him, while we wondered at the type of care he might receive in this far-away third world country.

Ready for the trip home, we gathered for breakfast the next morning and stared dumbfounded when our ill-fated Giardia riddled buddy appeared at the table. Pale and weak, he nonetheless was able to ambulate on his own and planned to fly out with us. A miracle?

No, our fellow MD trekker assured us. Just some cutting edge medication that was not available in the states. The doctor, an avid backpacker and trekker, well versed in wilderness illnesses and their medical treatment, reported our companion had been treated with a comparatively new antibiotic/medicine. It had been presented to our FDA, but had not been approved.

We said our "good-byes" at the airport, five first time trekkers who had bonded during our Nepalese odyssey. One remains a good friend, the other four are names in a journal. All memories, all a part of my life.

Chapter 2

Peru

ANDES DAY 1: AUGUST IN PERU

The sun rose as we flew high over the Andes, below us a spectacular panorama of towering snow-covered peaks bathed in the rosy light of daybreak, beyond the valley canyons still in deep purple shadows. I let my mind wander back over lines in the trip description, "a Trek through the Vilcabamba Range following an ancient footpath that remains the only means of access to the mountain region . . . crossing a spectacular pass between two glacier clad peaks," and wondered if I was looking at the path I'd take.

Landing at Cuzco, the ancient Incan capital of Peru's pre-Colombian empire, we were hurried through the small airport and past the vendors. There would be time later to appreciate the native crafts in the markets we'd visit. it was time now to rest and begin the adjustment to living at 11,200 feet above sea level.

Arriving at our hotel, we immediately were ushered to a table in the dining room-ostensibly for a brief orientation, in truth an introduction to "herbal tea." Instructed not to drink any more coffee or caffeine products, we were assured this coca tea would help us acclimatize to the altitude, and it would be our drink of choice for the next two weeks. A cup of an insipid pale green liquid was placed before each of us. Tasting it, I thought dried grass clippings from the yard back home infused in boiling water might give the same flavor. But, rules were rules, herbal tea it would be.

The next morning I nursed a grumbling headache as we boarded a van for the drive to the Sacred Valley of the Incas where we'd put in for a rafting trip on the Urubamba River. No white water, nothing wild, just some easy rapids as we floated past ancient villages that have changed little since Spanish colonial times.

As we sped along the narrow road to our put in spot, we passed a platoon of soldiers in camouflage, jogging along the shoulder of the road. The leader lowered the knobbed staff he carried as we approached them, and the men moved further into the roadside giving us wide berth. When questions were raised about why they were in this remote region, our guide answered "probably routine training exercises." We wondered aloud if they were looking for pockets of the dreaded Shining Path. That organization was a communist militant group. an off-shoot of the Communist Party of Peru. When founded in the 1980's, it aimed to replace the bourgeois democracy with a party of "The People."

The morning sun was warm as we finished putting the rafts in the river, and I decided to change into something more comfortable than the heavy cotton pants I was wearing. Grabbing a pair of shorts from my backpack, I walked up river over a shrubby rise to change.

As I sat tying my shoes, I heard the sound of footsteps, many footsteps, close by. Looking up, I saw not too far in the distance, the platoon of soldiers we had seen earlier, doing double-time down an embankment further upstream. I froze in disbelief. The knob atop the leader's staff was a human skull. The men made their way to the river, pulled off their boots, paired up and waded waist deep into the water. I held my breath as I watched each pair take turns holding the other's head under water till I thought my lungs would burst, then the head was released and the act was repeated on the other. (I learned later this exercise was done to build trust in each other.)

My mouth went dry, and my heart thudded, as I turned on my hands and knees and inched up through the bushes and over the small hill, then ran to the group waiting at the river. They stared at me in disbelief as I recounted what I'd just seen. The trip leader, absorbing what I had told them, gave the order to "Get out, now!" The words Shining Path were not uttered, but they hung heavy between us. The five trekkers were hurriedly loaded into one van with the guide and driver, we were off . . . so much for rafting the Urubamba.

The group's easy back and forth chatter that had filled our days was strangely missing as we drove away. I was lost in my own thoughts as the country side of the Sacred Valley of the Incas slipped by unnoticed till we arrived at Písac, an old fortress town and ruin. Perched high above the valley, there was an Incan burial site and a temple complex to explore, but only after climbing a narrow, maybe two-foot-wide trail, that hugged the mountainside and abruptly dropped off hundreds of feet. To climb or not to climb. I considered it briefly, then checked into my room at our overnight lodging, a lovely old hacienda.

It had been an unsettling day.

The next morning we drove on to Ollantaytambo. The trip prospectus described it as a "virtual living Inca village, retaining the stonework, narrow streets and family courtyards of that period." Indeed, the town and the colorfully dressed natives offered the feeling of being back in the fifteenth Century. After checking in to another lovely old hacienda, with a courtyard filled with flowers, we set off to explore the ruins. It was an impressive ceremonial site, one of the only major Inca victories against the Spanish. I half listened as the guide related the history. My head throbbing, I sat down, leaned against the ancient rock work and let the others scurry among the dust of antiquity. Returning to the hotel, I excused myself from dinner. In spite of pain medication, Diamox for altitude sickness, and nasal inhalants, my headache had reached a blinding point. My head felt as though it was slowly being tightened in a vise.

The following morning, as we packed to depart for the trailhead, I made the painful decision to cancel my trip. I simply couldn't stand the pain any longer, and began to wonder if I had a brain tumor. It was time to go home.

I gave the news to our guide, he nodded in agreement, then suggested I go to the hotel's small infirmary room for oxygen, and perhaps temporary relief. Obviously many tourists found help in the line of green oxygen tanks that were stored against the back wall.

Adjusting the mask on my face, I inhaled for about a half hour, then, head still pounding, made my way across the courtyard toward the main office to arrange my return to the states.

As I crossed the cobblestones the fragrance of coffee, maybe freshly ground, maybe freshly brewed, hit my senses. I decided I might as well have a cup or two, no more herbal tea. I was leaving the trek, I'd make my own choices.

After sipping several cups and no more than fifteen minutes later, the headache began to subside, as if a magic wand had been waved over me. I realized I had been suffering caffeine withdrawal, as bad I'm told, as that of hard drugs.

(Researching this reaction on my return home, I found that regular caffeine consumption reduces sensitivity to caffeine. When caffeine intake is reduced, the body becomes oversensitive to adenosine, a type of chemical that circulates in our bloodstream. In response to this over sensitiveness, blood pressure drops dramatically, causing an excess of blood in the head (though not necessarily on the brain), leading to a headache. This headache, well known among coffee drinkers, usually lasts from one to five days, and can be alleviated with analgesics such as aspirin. It is also alleviated with caffeine intake.) Yes!

After filling my canteen with strong, black coffee, I hurriedly rejoined the group. With caffeine surging thorough my blood stream and a smile within my heart, I waited while the contents of the van were rearranged, for my seat space had already been assigned to a box of supplies. Finally, everything was packed, the cargo on the van's top rack was lashed down, and trekkers, guides, camp crew squeezed together for take-off.

Togetherness on a rocky road in Peru, we drove about four hours to our first camp beyond Mollepata. According to the trip's description, our trek of fifty miles, beginning here in the sheltered plateau of the high-altitude valley, would take us past the tree line through the sparse vegetation of the *páramo*, then on to the dry grassland of the Andean *puna,* before skirting, at 15,600 feet, the huge glacial moraine at the foot of Mt. Salcantay. Descending from those icy heights, we'd trek through the *puna* once more, before reaching the traditional bush land that precedes the mountainous "eyebrow of the jungle." In that tropical forest the trip promised us hummingbirds, parrots, and orchids.

Cruising slowly across the *altiplano*, a windy plateau at 11,500 feet, we all seemed lost in our own thoughts, just absorbing our whereabouts, the rather rocky, barren country side, small towns and little farms. I noticed fences of cactus growing in the red volcanic soil, and compared them to the Crown of Thorn fences I had seen growing in Nepal. Native-grown ingenuity, both obviously effective in corralling cattle.

Those cactus fences prompted me to remember an article read long ago about the Aztecs, Incas and the cochineal insect that eats cactus. This tiny bug that hides in a cottony fuzz, produces red dye, a dye so brilliant that (if old records are to be believed), after Herman Cortés entered Mexico and discovered the source of the hue, he sent samples home to Spain as one of the wonders of the New World. History tells us that by 1600 cochineal was second only to silver as the most valuable export from Mexico.

We stopped to stretch our legs near a lone farm, a couple of small stone structures covered with thatched roofs standing rather forlornly, like lone sentinels on the hillside. Time for a shot or two of my drug of choice, black coffee, an energy bar and a look around.

While some mangy dogs watched from a distance, a lone rooster came strutting toward us across the rock strewn pasture, and, as if given a signal, each of us reached for our cameras. For before us was a bird to put a parrot to shame, a creation that would no doubt have left Dr. Seuss speechless! Under the bright red comb, the bird had a fringe of buff colored feathers, this atop vermillion neck feathers that abruptly ended or sat atop a body of speckled black and white feathers. The wings were snow white. Beyond its rear feathers of light yellow, was a fan-like tail of iridescent blue-green.

I wondered if the early Aztecs ceremonial dress could have been inspired by this bird, and created by what that tiny cactus bug could offer. For where do ideas spring from? Sketches and paintings in history books show the Incan with feathered head dresses, their warrior's shields, women's faces and breasts dyed red, a color that had the same significance to Inca's as purple did to European royalty.

Driving on, as we rounded a curve, the bus came alive with excitement, for in the far, far distance, snow covered peaks came into view, the land of Machu Picchu, where our trek would end fifty miles and five days later.

We left our bus and driver at Mollepata and hiked for an hour or so to our campsite, where horses, mules and some willing strong backs were waiting to lead us on. But that was tomorrow. I pushed my duffle bag inside the small tent, and In the solitude of that quiet space, I offered the gods a Thank You! For though the climb was steep, the air was thin, and my breath was short, my head was clear. I sang a silent Hallelujah, I was trekking in Peru.

The next afternoon I sat beside a rocky trail that snaked up the mountain side, winded and tired, staring at the valley below and assessing my situation. It was the middle of September, I was not in the jungles of Borneo, I was climbing the Peruvian Andes. I had not trained for a high mountain trek; I was exhausted and winded in this thin air. This was far more than I had bargained for when I hurriedly changed trip plans, and I wondered how I'd make it over a 17,000 foot pass that loomed a week away. Or if I wanted to even try.

Back in February, Earthwatch, a non-profit environmental organization had accepted my credentials, and I'd signed up for a three week assignment working with Dr. Bruite Galdikas on an Indonesian Orangutan project, deep in the jungles of Borneo. These man-like creatures had interested me since I was a kid, and the chance to be in the presence of and to work with a distinguished scientist like Galdikas was an exciting thought, a chance of a life time.

I'd studied the geography of Borneo, the history, the indigenous peoples, the wildlife. I was familiar with the mountains, the beaches, and the rivers. I'd had my jungle shots. My jungle clothes, bug repellant and mosquito netting were packed, and I was ready to ride up the river in a dugout canoe to the Orangutan Camp. Up before dawn, I'd be led through a swampy, mucky forest by flashlight, watch the orangs leave their nests, monitor their feeding patterns, follow them all day till they build a new nests each evening. I'd spend most of the time looking up, all the time being aware of "annoying leeches, biting fire ants and poisonous snakes."

I'd made notes that some of the wild orangs object to human observers: they might scream at us, hurl branches, or even try to defecate on those below. After a few days of those activities, we'd trade with volunteers in the camp, and observe and play with baby orangs or those that had been captives.

Then the phone call from Earthwatch that changed everything. It came to me in Tampa on a hot and muggy July afternoon. "We have reports the tribal unrest has broken out in the jungle. We feel your safety would be compromised; therefore the trip is cancelled."

O.K. I'd come to terms with the fact that travel to Borneo was out . . . but my calendar had been cleared, those three weeks had been set aside for travel, I would not be daunted, I'd find a place to go.

I continued to sit there on the side of the mountain, reflecting on my decision to travel in Peru, to set my sights on a valley between two towering glacier clad peaks, Mt. Salcantay (20,574 feet) and Mt. Humantay (19,239 feet) Thumbing through a catalog from the company that had arranged my trek in Nepal several years earlier, my eye hit on a page that offered "A Trek in Peru" in the time frame I'd planned on using. After a day in Lima, I'd fly to Cuzco and spend a couple days acclimatizing to the altitude (11.200 feet) then a day exploring the Ollantaytambo ruins, then on to raft the Urubamba. Finally a drive to the remote valley of Maliputo where we'd meet our camp crew and pack animals to begin our trek "through alpine meadows toward Mt. Salcantay."

Perfect! Didn't I walk four miles every morning? Hadn't I just come back from my home in the mountains of North Carolina where I was accustomed to climbing hills and mountain trails? Yep, this was gonna be a piece of cake. Reservations made, pre-departure information hurriedly scanned equipment no problem, duffle bags, backpack, clothing and boots, had it all. I was off to Peru and a grand adventure.

I'd noticed the attention the company gave to ACM or Acute Mountain Sickness . . . which is evidenced by headache, extreme fatigue, loss of appetite, swelling of ankles or eyelids, but had given it little thought. The lines "unless you are experienced at hiking above 15,000 feet, do not treat this trek lightly," came back to haunt me that morning as I struggled with a decision to keep on trekking . . . or just admit defeat and go back down.

As the words "keep on" crossed my mind, I thought about a couple of dark times in my life when I didn't think I had the strength to go on. But I'd kept on, persevered, and beat those tough times.

Pulling on the strength that got me through those difficult days, I picked myself up ready to start the climb, when one of the native guides walked back carrying a walking stick he'd cut for me. I watched as he peeled back the silvery-gray bark, disclosing a pale yellow wood. He shortened it a bit, gratefully I took it in hand and we climbed on, finally catching up with the rest.

Our camp for the night was nestled in a rock-strewn meadow surrounded by small hills, deep in the cradle of

Mt. Salcantay and Mt. Huayanay whose snow-covered peaks loomed above us. As whipped as I was, I deposited my backpack, and climbed a short distance before dinner just to drink in the landscape and photograph those magnificent summits. Our green tents were assembled in a half circle in the field, beside a glacier-fed river, its milky-blue water tumbling over the river bed. The horses and mules were tethered in the field, smoke curled from a camp fire; our little group had made this camp a home for the night.

I reveled in the return of an appetite that urged me on to the cook tent, where dinner was waiting; the simple feast on the table was one to remember. My journal indicates that chicken and sliced avocado were served. Then it rhapsodizes in the potato dish set before us: pounded, beaten or mashed potatoes to which the cook had added a bit of olive oil, the squeeze of fresh lime juice and a dash of hot-pepper, food for the Gods. I ate till satiated, said "good night" and crawled into my tent to ponder the trip's events, from the horror of a human skull to the delight of mashed potatoes. I slept the sleep of the just.

The next morning we faced a day of climbing, maybe eight hours or more on a narrow, rocky trail. Our itinerary indicated that part of the time we'd follow the aqueduct that the Incas built to bring water to the valley. Fortified with concrete today, it still served to remind us of man's ingenuity.

The going was slow for me. These were not the gentle mountains of North Carolina, this was a big time climb. To lighten the load, I'd pared the contents of my backpack to the bare necessities: my canteen, a couple energy bars, hand soap, toilet tissue, small bottles of bug repellent and sun screen. My wet wash cloth was pinned to a strap on the pack, so it could flutter and dry during the day, a trick I'd learned on the trek in Nepal.

The walk soon turned into a hard slog. I dropped to the rear of the line with a guide and began concentrating on just putting one foot in front of the other as we climbed, at times, it seemed straight up. Straight up, as in a wall straight up, with hairpin switch backs thrown in for a challenge. The horses with riders and mules with packs passed us, they too seemed to be aware of the difficult trail, lowering their gaze to the ground and carefully putting one hoof in front of the other, winding slowly toward the promised pass. The bells on their harness rang softly, a tinkle and a jingle for each step, a lovely melody to focus on as we pushed higher.

Watching the animals pass, I became aware of a red hat on a mule's head, Its long ears poked through slits the muleteer had cut in the crown, and a couple of colorful ribbons tied at the band. I put my hand up to check my trademark red felt fedora, and smiled at the whimsy that brightened the moment.

Suddenly, one of the caballeros turned his horse around, rode back to me, dismounted, and said, "Cuántos años tiene [How old are you]?"
I replied, "Cincuenta y ocho [Fifty-eight]," and asked, "y tu [And you]?"
He stared at me for a moment and said,
"Veinte ocho [Twenty-eight]." Then with a firm voice he ordered, "Tu manejas [You use]."

Thankfully I got up in the saddle and began the steep ascent again, grateful for a young man's considerate assessment of my difficult struggle.

All was well, I relaxed, happy to be free, to just look. and be, as we climbed. Maybe half an hour later I let my glance drop down a few hundred feet into the canyon on my right and to my horror saw the skeleton of a horse. Or maybe a mule. I didn't know and didn't care; it had four long legs and was a pile of bones and I was getting off the horse and taking my chances that my two legs would get me to that promised land.

An improbable landscape greeted us as we reached the summit. I thought, *if there is life on the moon, the gardens there might look like this.* Small rosettes of light and dark green lichen covered some of the gray granite; here and there tiny coral cylinders snuggled against the rocky crevices. Long feathery blades of dry green grass grew beside a velvety, smoky, grey-green vine, whose long leaves crawled up the dark gray rocks like octopus tentacles.

Shrugging off my backpack, I put it down, used it a pillow and stared at the sky, thinking now it's going to be downhill. I knew it would be both up and down, but after the last couple of days I figured the "ups" would be a piece of cake as we descended into lower altitudes, and another kind of environment. After leaving the barren mountains we'd just climbed, the travel company's trip description showed that we'd descend into the "eyebrow of the jungle" and finally see the promised hummingbirds, parrots and orchids. I was ready. I fell asleep and dreamed a technicolor dream of pinks and purple and yellows.

A light frost covered the ground the next morning, it was winter here at our 15,000 foot campsite. Packing my duffle, I fingered a pair of shorts at the bottom of the bag, and wondered if tomorrow I could shed the heavy cargo pants I'd worn for three days.

Leaving the moonscape of our camp, we began our trek on the eastern slope of the continental cordillera, heading for the little village of St. Theresa where we'd catch the train for an hours ride to Machu Picchu. It would be a two day trek down into valley, a deep cleft in the earth maybe a thousand feet below us.

The name Santa Theresa became emblazoned on our consciousness. It was the small town where we'd catch the train to Machu Picchu, a couple of days away; the valley we'd hike down; and the river by the same name, a silvery thread that wove its way down the mountains, hundreds, maybe thousands of feet from our path.

Rounding a switchback, I caught my first glimpse of the river, a glittering ribbon on the floor of the valley. Andean condors glided silently on the air currents, dipping and turning as if they heard the tunes of a Strauss waltz. The vegetation was showing signs of the season's change, spring blooms beginning to bud and flower. I caught sight of several straggly plants of the same Joe Pye weed that grew along stream banks and meadows back home, and then a big bush of Scotch broom came into view. While we stopped to photograph the fans of yellow sweet pea-like flowers, one of the Indian guides walked up beside us and touched first the plant, then his heart. Eyes sparkling, he spoke quickly in Quechua, his native tongue. We got the message that this plant had obvious significance. We were hard pressed to understand him, until our interpreter translated-- the native people use the plant as a heart tonic, one of its properties being a diuretic, used to control high blood pressure.

Picking my way through the small boulders that made the descent a force to be reckoned with, I realized an opportunity I'd never considered on this journey. Until then, I'd directed my energies to just putting one foot in front of the other and finishing the day's climb. Now, enjoying an easier descent through the sparse vegetation, I could delve further into the medicines of an indigenous people.

I'd become fascinated with the medicinal properties of plants when I first began to spend summers in western North Carolina. The area we lived in was still populated by descendants of the early settlers, hiking together they began to share their knowledge of medicinal plants and their mountain remedies with this flat lander. Yarrow, sweet birch, sumac, yellow root, and jewel weed were among many that took on a new meaning when they caught my eye as we walked the trails.

Acknowledging my interest in herbal medicine, our interpreter asked the Indian guide to point out medicinal plants to me, and from then on, he walked with me, sharing a pharmacy of the Andes. The sun was warm on my body as we wound our way to the valley, stopping now and then to examine a plant. We stopped by sage, an herb I quickly recognized for it grew in my garden, and the native pulled several leaves from the plant, rolled them in his fingers and indicated I should inhale. Suddenly its sharp odor took me back to a November day in my grandmother's kitchen, filled with the Thanksgiving Day fragrance of roast turkey, its stuffing seasoned with sage.

Here in the Andes, the medicine man indicated sage is used to treat respiratory ailments, coughs, colds sore throats. Before the trek ended, our Indian guide shared more ... farther down the mountain I found a familiar leaf, one I'd known since childhood. A rounded leaf with veins or lines radiating from a vague center, the nasturtium leaf had reminded me of a spider. Back home daring hostesses would tuck the little, spicy red and yellow blooms here and there on a luncheon plate of chicken salad, the more adventuresome would nibble on them, assuring all they were safe. Indeed they were, for the ancients, and not so ancients, used an infusion of the leaves as a disinfectant and wound healer.

Ahead of us the steep, rocky, trail stretched as far as the eye could see, then faded away into a hillside of dark green vegetation. Down, down into the valley, we slowly wound our way along the narrow path, when suddenly we came to an abrupt halt at a log crossing over a rushing stream. Now picking my way up and down steep rock-strewn mountain trails was one thing; balancing myself on a log over a swift river was another. Sharp rocks lined the slope to the water's edge, but with the hillside's pitch almost straight up and down, there was no other way across. I made a note this wasn't in the trip description and then pushed negativity out of my mind, took the proverbial deep breath and began to inch my way across. "Don't look down," I told myself, yet in the next breath I said "but you have to." Ignoring everything but my boots and the log, I began to move slowly, foot by cautious foot. Reaching the other side, I offered thanks to the gods that be, for safe deliverance.

Slowly we phased into another climate zone. New growth emerged beside tangled, dried winter vines, buds swelled on bare branches; and daffodil like blooms clustered among the dry grasses. Further on, my glance landed on an orchid plant, its spray of small rosy-purple blooms splayed out beside a lichen covered boulder, reminded me of butterflies.

In a meadow far above the Salcantay River, we made camp. A small farmhouse sat in the distance, a large rosebush bloomed beside part of an old rail fence, our first sight of habitation in days. Two little girls with serious faces came out to take inventory of us, their solemn eyes staring at what . . . our pale skin, bare legs and backpacks? The little yellow dog that had followed us for a few days, danced around the kids begging to be petted.

Ambling along the trail the next day, we rounded a curve and were greeted by an older man with a colorful shawl draped around his shoulders, an old, jaunty fedora atop his head. He held a chipped, white enamel pan piled high with small boiled potatoes, and with a smile he offered the plate toward us. I took one, bit into it, and to my surprise the flesh was a purplish blue. As the others reached for some, his face broke out in a bigger grin and he bowed slightly as we offered our thanks.

(Later I learned that there are many flesh colors of the potato, whose birthplace is in South America. There is scientific evidence that potatoes were domesticated as early as 10,000 years ago in the High Andes of southeastern Peru and northwestern Bolivia.)

We trekked through the tropical forest along the valley floor, following the river to the village of Santa Teresa where we would catch the train to Machu Picchu. Our world came alive with life and color; there were trees covered with bright orange and purple blooms, orchids, hibiscus, banana trees. Butterflies and hummingbirds floated and danced among them, while scarlet macaws and parakeets squawked and chirped from their perches among the tree branches, maybe protesting our presence, perhaps welcoming us.

Finally, crossing an old suspension bridge (with some planks missing) we arrived in Santa Teresa, and headed for the train station and our ride to Machu Picchu. Narrow gauge rail tracks passed close to the large stone steps that curved in front of the rail station, serving as pedestals for the passengers that waited there. Natives lounged beside their large bundles, some parcels tied in what looked like old bedsheets, some bundled in bright, colorful serapes. A crate with three chickens rested next to baskets of produce bound for the markets in Cuzco and a heap of duffle bags attested to our presence.

The train pulled in, our guides helped us load our duffle bags, and the moment came for bittersweet goodbyes. We piled on board and found every seat taken, even the aisles were crowded with natives on their way to Cuzco. I directed a smile at a couple of women sitting beside their bundles, questioning with my eyes and hands; they understood and moved over a bit as I wedged my duffle bag into that small vacated space, and used it as a seat for the hour's ride.

In Cuzco, a dusty bus was waiting to take us on to Machu Picchu, to a hotel with hot showers and real beds. The travel company had stated in its trip description that we'd, "have a chance to explore the ancient city before the hordes of tourists arrived on the morning train," a chance I'd not appreciated until shortly after dawn. I saw the deserted city Hiram Bingham saw in 1911 when he made the discovery. "Lost" since the fifteenth century and so well hidden by the towering jungle-covered walls of the Cordillera Vilcabamba, it was never discovered by the Spaniards. It seemed a true picture of what the Inca world must have been like. A sacred city built without the help of a metal tool.

On a guided walk I learned the Incas were engineers without parallel in the New World, fitting the huge stones of white granite in the construction so carefully together that mortar was unnecessary. Magnificent temples and several hundred buildings of elaborate stonework dominated the scene; thousands of steps connected the ancient city's sections. Agricultural terraces were cut into the mountains for farming, the soil used in those terraces carried up in baskets from the Urubamba Valley, over 1,300 feet below.

One of the world's greatest archaeologic sites, it still holds the secret of its creation and abandonment.

Keepin' On, Walkin' On

Chapter 3

Pakistan

PAKISTAN-SILK ROAD

As we followed the ancient Silk Road, trekking across western China on our way to the Hunza Valley in Pakistan, an avalanche on the Karakorum Highway near the Khunjerab Pass forced us to halt and reroute. On our return to an air base at Ürümqi, our outfitter had offered us a choice: fly into Islamabad and take what we could find or return to Beijing. Five of us chose a roll of the dice and a flight into Islamabad.

Hours later, in a small dark office, somewhere in the fabled old city, we sipped hot tea while pouring over maps and possible routes. At last we chose the chance to travel to the tribal lands of NW Pakistan. With two jeeps, two drivers, two guards armed with AK 47's and a warning that if we left the main roads of Pakistan, none of their national laws would protect us. It was explained to us that years earlier Pakistan granted nearly 40,000 square miles of land to the Pathans, a fierce warlike people, who ruled the territory with their own code of honor, one that knows no compromise. Men value that code more than life, and women live their lives in a system called *purdah*, hidden from the outside world while covered in cloth from head to toe. While professing to understand the seriousness of this culture, we took a leap of faith into a land and an adventure that would test us all.

Leaving Islamabad, we traveled north toward the Swat Valley, choosing to camp along the Indus River that first evening. Thousands of stars lit the ink black sky as I walked along the banks before turning in, trying hard to remember this river's place in ancient history, but with no luck.

After I returned home I browsed encyclopedias, learning that a thriving civilization existed there along about the time of the Egyptian and Mesopotamian states. While other civilizations were devoting huge amounts of time and resources to the rich, the mystical, and the dead, Indus Valley inhabitants were taking a practical approach to their lives, supporting the common, living people. They built irrigation systems and farmed crops of wheat, cotton, and

barley. While they believed in an afterlife and employed a
system of social divisions, they also believed resources
were more valuable in circulation among the living than on
display or buried underground. Evidence of early
environmentalists?

Next we drove on to the Swat Valley, and spent two
nights in a marble palace, better known as the Swat Serena
Hotel, finding the transition from sleeping bag to an
innerspring mattress an easy one. The hotel, built in the
1920's and situated on acres of beautifully manicured
lawns, had hosted Queen Elizabeth, who described the area
as the Switzerland of Asia.

Taking advantage of free time to amble through the
gardens and grounds, I found myself near the laundry

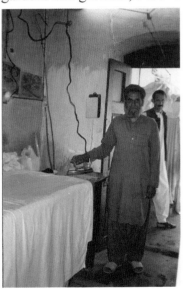
where sheets were drying on
clotheslines in the hot
sunshine. Ignoring the advice
I'd been given about not
making eye contact with
men, I approached a fellow
who was hanging towels,
and with my eyes, a smile
and hand gestures, I inquired
about seeing the laundry
itself. He understood, and
showed me into a small
room where large galvanized
tubs of soapy hot water
bubbled on a stove, while the contents were stirred about
by an attendant holding a large stick. In another area sheets

were being ironed by hand, the fellow with a large black iron in his hand, proudly showed me how he folded each piece. I felt quite safe there in that primitive laundry, and when I turned down the bed covers that evening, appreciated the care that had gone into the fresh white sheets.

Continuing north through the Swat Valley, a beautiful Alpine like area, our jeeps carried us on narrow, rocky roads along rivers and through villages at the base of the mountains to the town of Chitral, with occasional stops for a stretch, photographs or prayers. At an appointed hour, we'd pull to the side of the road, the drivers and guards would exit the jeeps with their prayer rugs and AK-47s, then, facing Mecca, they laid down their guns, spread the rugs and knelt in prayer. Then it was "on the road again."

It was an amazing ride, with a look at a people and a way of life that seemed incomprehensible in the late 20th Century. Along rivers, water wheels ground grain. In a small village a snake handler held the writhing reptiles above his head in a crowd of men and boys. There was little sight of women along the way, their world seemed to be restricted to life behind high mud walls in the family compound. Occasionally we'd see women sitting along the road that we shared with donkey carts, they appeared as mounds of black cloth. Even though their eyes were covered with a black mesh, they would turn their faces as we approached. In the market places only men and children held shopping bags as they shopped for their families provisions.

Weeks later, flying from Islamabad to Bangkok on my way home, a Pakistani Army officer sat beside me, a doctor who had been home on leave for several months. Learning of my travels through the Northwest Region, he asked me what I thought about his country, saying I was quite privileged to have been in that part of the land. I replied something like "The countryside was beautiful, the people hospitable . . . but I thought the women were so isolated, so sequestered living their lives behind walls in those adobe compounds, cut off from the world . . . I thought women needed to have freedom, and something outside the compound to dream about." He looked at me, thought for a moment and said, "My dear, our women do dream. They dream about having enough food, they dream of safety and health for their children and happiness for their families; obviously, my dear, they do dream."

Pow! He really put it to me, didn't he!

Leaving the Swat Valley we drove on to the town of Chitral, located high on a plateau in the Hindu Kush range of mountains that lie between Afghanistan and Pakistan. The snow covered summit of Tirich Mir, the highest peak in the range, overlooks the town, and was easily seen from the police station, where we stopped to present credentials and apply for a permit to enter the Kalash Valley. Though it was a town of one dusty street, Chitral boasted another fine hotel, and, to our surprise, and my delight, a polo field, the Shandur Polo Grounds, billed as the highest polo field in the world at 12,200 feet above sea level.

When we checked into the hotel, we learned a match was scheduled for later that afternoon, and "yes," those of us that wished to attend, were welcome.

Driving out to the polo field, our guide again reminded us of our special guest status in that part of the world and cautioned us to do nothing to attract attention to ourselves. Didn't seem to be a general problem, but later proved hard for me. I'd grown up on a horse, and while I never played polo, that afternoon I let the game pick me up and carry me with the horses, riders, mallets and ball to the goal. Forgetting caution, I stood and cheered the team I'd chosen to root for; heads in the open air bleachers swiveled, dark eyes bore into me, then turned indifferently away and back to the match.

We were shown the utmost courtesy after the match, as we walked out onto the field and among the horses and riders, with cameras in hand, recording more serendipitous moments in a land where cultures could, and did, easily clash.

Early the following morning, as I left my room for breakfast, I was handed a lesson in exercising slow and cautionary movements. I nodded a "Good Morning" to the armed guard who stood at the end of the hall below the Exit sign, just a couple doors down from mine. His face remained expressionless as though I didn't exist. A few steps down the hallway, I remembered some papers I needed for the front desk, and whipped around to go back. Just as suddenly, the fierce-eyed guard had taken several steps forward, his gun pointed at my chest. I came to a halt, smiled a weak smile and with key in hand motioned to my door. After a few seconds that seemed an eternity, he lowered his gun and nodded to me. I had the go-ahead, while pin-prickles of sweat broke out under my arm pits.

The news at the breakfast table was good; we had been cleared to enter the Valley of the Kalash, and would leave at daybreak the next morning. Though the village was only twenty-five miles away, it would take at least three hours of travel over a narrow, torturous road, straight up the mountain to the village of Rumbur, where, we had been told, the people lived in a culture foreign to the customs and religion of Pakistan.

The next day I sat wedged in the rear seat of the jeep with two other intrepid souls, struggling to keep my eyes shut as we snaked around another rocky turn on a steep mountain road better fashioned for donkey carts. Wishing hard that I hadn't taken the window seat that was my draw, I now clung to it. The compulsion to close my eyes to the abyss on the side seemed irresistible, but ignoring it was impossible as we crawled along the narrow road, maybe 2000 feet above the Rumbur River chasm, one hairpin turn after another. We were on our way to a secluded valley high in the Hindu Kush, to meet the Kalash, a light skinned, blue eyed people who were thought to be direct descendants of the Greek-Macedonian armies who invaded this region in the fourth century B.C.

The road seemed a metaphor for my life during the past days. After abrupt changes and dangerous curves in the chaos of the Karakorams, detoured on a long planned and well established, safe itinerary, now the jeep was carrying us to a corner of the world I didn't know existed, with laws and customs that seemed incomprehensible, and, if I thought long enough about them, quite frightening.

We entered the small village of Rambur, and found ourselves in another world. Gone were the women encased in black garments, whose eyes looked at the world through black mesh. Here the women's faces were open, we were welcomed by shy smiles, dancing eyes and laughter as they crowded around our jeeps.

Their bodies were covered in long black gowns richly embroidered with bright designs of red, yellow, purple and green. Small similarly colored pillbox hats were perched atop their heads, ropes of bright beads hung around their necks, with cowry shells visible on some strands, rings adorned their fingers and bracelets jingled on their arms.

The village square was crowded with the curious, their smiles heartwarming, and they welcomed us as we ambled around the village. The architectural style of the homes, stacked one above another like steps up the mountain side, reminded me somewhat of early settler homes in our Southwest. The hills were rocky and rather barren, with trees scattered sparsely up the steep sides. We caught sight of several young shepherd girls with their flocks of goats among the trees.

Gathering our backpacks and lunches from the jeeps, we found a spot to picnic in a small glade of trees, and were soon joined by the local schoolmaster, a scholarly man wearing a jaunty beret and sporting horn-rimmed glasses. He spoke limited English, but patiently tried to answer our many questions about this land and its people, who seemed to defy identity with other Pakistanis just down the mountain road, some miles away. As gentle breezes drifted through the trees, so did strains of music, for down on the square a couple of young boys began to play their flutes and drums. After lunch we went to join them. The richly garbed women and girls began to dance their slow steps, a few bystanders clapped softly in rhythm and swayed in time with the melodies.

All too soon it was time to leave this Shangri-La in the Hindu Kush, and return to the somber, restrictive world of Pakistan by way of that torturous, twisting road to Chitral where we would catch a small plane to Peshawar, a large metropolitan city near the eastern end of the Khyber Pass.

As we drove out to the famed Pass, an integral part of the ancient Silk Road, we looked down into Afghanistan and watched an ancient tractor pulling five or six wagons piled high with refugee's belongings, while the people walked alongside. They were crossing into Pakistan, for even though the Afghan war with Russia was over, the promise of a better life seemed to be over the border.

A few days later we drove from Peshawar down another narrow, dusty road to the town of Darra Adam Khel, described to us as the gun capital of the world. Traveling toward a side road we were stopped by a heavy chain, with links of forged steel as big around as my wrist. Our driver/guard/guide engaged in dialogue with a fierce looking fellow who stood guard at the dirt lane leading from the main road. At last the padlock was undone, we were allowed to pass. We proceeded on our way to the gun makers and markets of Darra, a town of one main street lined with closet sized shops that produce guns. A town beyond comprehension, a town that will be forever burned into memory.

Dozens of small gun shops lined the street. Men, some sitting on the dirt floors, using hand tools and primitive lathes, were fashioning copies of well-known rifles, pistols and machine guns. Most weapons had been sold to the Afghans fighting the Russians, but although that war was over, the demand for guns remained high among the Pakistanis.

As I stood watching the gunsmiths work, another moment of a never-to-be-forgotten moment was thrust upon me. While standing outside the shop, and as our guard chatted with the gunsmiths, one of the men thrust an AK-47 into my hands and through the interpreter asked if I wanted to shoot. I smiled, shook my head no and replied "no thanks." With that he took the gun from my hands, put it to his shoulder, pulled the trigger and blasted off into the air above the mountain side. Then he turned and smiled at me.

Keepin' On, Walkin' On

Chapter 4

Kamchatka

KAMCHATKA '93

The expedition to Kamchatka was a go. In August 1993, one of the leading outfitters in the United States had been granted permission for an expedition to visit one of the last great wildernesses in the world, and I had a place on it.

Kamchatka, in Russia's Far East, off limits to the rest of the world until the collapse of the Soviet Union, held the promise of high adventure. We were to helicopter to the River Zhupanova, hike four days through the *taiga*, or boreal forest, to a secret treasure, the Valley of the Geysers. Dotted with volcanos and geothermal activity, the valley was another Yellowstone, but with no roads and no crowds. Then, after being transported back to the Zhupavona, we were to raft four days down that wild river, through lands that were home to Siberian bighorns, sables, marmots, and the prize sighting, "*Ursus Arctos*," the biggest brown bears on the continent. And we'd witness the fall run of the beautiful red Coho Salmon. Late August into September, a perfect season, clear warm days, cool nights.

This well planned, perfect trip began to unravel at the airport in Anchorage, when our guides met us with the news that the Russian company they had contracted with had backed out of their agreement. We would be put in the hands of members of a hunter and fishermen's club in the country north of the capital city of Petropavlovsk. They would see to our safety and comfort, though certainly not in the style we had been sold. We watched as hastily purchased folding camp chairs were arranged with our luggage, one for each of us! I wondered where the hunters and fishermen would sit.

On the plane over the Bering Sea, we received more unsettling news. A typhoon had been raging in the Pacific, and the sunny skies we had planned to trek under were being replaced with low hanging gray clouds and heavy rain. We were being diverted from Petropavlovsk, and flying on to Magadan, a port city in far east Russia on the sea of Okhotsk. From there we would board an Aeroflot charter, then fly to our destination Petropavlovsk. Which a couple of wags began referring to as "Peter and Paul" or "P&P" because, after all, back in 1740, the Danish explorer Vitus Bering had named the city he founded after his ships, the St. Peter and St. Paul.

An Aeroflot Charter flight . . . those few words caught me in a web of memories, and I offered a quick prayer. A few years before, while on a trip across Siberia with a delegation of Sierra Club members, we had caught a late night charter flight from Moscow to Abakan. As I watched fellow passengers boarding the plane, I noticed their carry-ons. It appeared just about anything one could hold in their arms or stuff in a pocket was fair game; food, an open bottle of liquor stuffed in a coat chest pocket, a small roll of carpets, a wood sculpture and an ancient wicker carrier with a very unhappy cat. Somewhere, east of the Ural Mountains, the cat got out of its carrier, causing near panic as it ricocheted through the cabin, down the aisle, over seat backs, terrifying a member of our group who had a deathly fear of cats. My prayer was simple, "Please God, no more surprises today."

Our group of eight adventurers were collected, watched over, and led by a young man who was getting his Ph. D. in Slavic Linguistics at M.I.T. He was frowning as we finally gathered in the airport after an uneventful flight across the Kamchatka peninsula under overcast skies. With an eye on the approaching storm, the schedule had been thrown into complete disarray. We'd spend the night in Petropavlovsk, leave early the next morning, not for the river, but for the Valley of the Geysers, flying there while visibility was good. We would then trek. "Yes" he ruefully admitted, "probably in the rain, but we do have rain gear, don't we!" And finally a week later, the weather gods permitting, we would raft, not the Zhupanova, but the Bystraya that flowed south to the Sea of Okhotsk.

Well, there went my weeks of map studies, done so I'd be oriented to the land, the route of rivers, knowing full well where I was during the expedition. Leaving the gray, cement block airport to board an exhaust-belching, lumbering bus, I passed windows covered with curtains made of a mesh like material, with big butterflies woven into them. "What contrast," I thought, "cement blocks and fragile butterfly wings." Either someone had a sense of humor or a need to remember that this world is not all dull, square and rigid.

We overnighted in another square gray block building, the clean and spartan Oktyabrskaya Hotel. After a hurried breakfast, (the rain clouds were moving in) we took off in a MI 8 helicopter for the Valley of the Geysers, about two and a half hours north. The valley lies in the Kronotsky Nature Reserve, a UNESCO Natural World Heritage Property, and is the second largest geyser field in the world after Yellowstone. Because no fish swim in the Geyser River, early explorers were discouraged from following the course of the river upstream, keeping the valley a secret until 1941, when It was discovered by Tatyana Ustinova, a hydrologist exploring the gorge-like valley with a guide from the Itleman tribe. Findings were published fourteen years later, but there were no explorations until 1972, and no foreign visitors until after the fall of the Soviet Union 1991,

Landing under threatening gray skies, it seemed as if we had entered an enchanted land, where nature's forces were baring themselves. Several hundred geysers spouted in multiple tiers along the slopes of the small valley, boiling caldrons of mud bubbled here and there, while ground water seeping from azure pools of water returned to the surface as hissing steam.

Those sky-blue pools of water were surrounded by a carpet of deep green ground cover, plants that flourished in the warmth and dampness. The landscape was in perpetual motion. Coursing through the rough boulders that had been tossed here and there by volcanic action was a stream. Too small to be a river, too big to be a creek, it rushed along, tossing waves of white water before it.

The valley scene was mesmerizing, a misty, ethereal landscape of unending motion. Sitting on a bench overlooking a ravine, watching the movement below, I was reminded of a symphony orchestra. The little short bursts of steam for the reeds, the bubbling caldrons of steaming mud were the drum rolls, the sassy short geyser bursts comprised the brass section, and the river running through the valley was the string section. Somewhere in there was a Conductor, and I imagined him calling in first this section, then the next. Each performed its part, then suddenly came the crescendo, the mightiest play of all. The geyser Velican shoots a plume twenty-thirty meters into the air, then a jet of steam up to three hundred meters reaches for the heavens. Slowly the action diminishes to a final hush, the conductor lowers his baton, and the observer sits transfixed till the song of a bird reminds one that the show is over, the next performance to begin in five to seven hours.

Ignoring threatening skies, our Russian hosts motioned to a wooden picnic table, inviting us to lunch with them: black bread, smoked fish, caviar, and sour cream, washed down with kvass, (a fermented beverage made from rye bread) vodka or strong black tea and blessed with toasts of "good voyage, happy wishes and come back to see us."

Food and friendship helped fortify us for the long trip ahead.

Invigorated, we flew out in a fine mist, landing quickly to drop off group number one at the river. Bad weather was closing in, and after two attempts to drop us in the Nalychevo Valley to begin our trek, the pilot gave a shrug and a "*nyet*" then turned the chopper back to a heliport outside Petropavlovsk.

"When the weather clears, we'll take off." His message was firm and clear. We settled back on benches under the eaves of a gray, concrete block building with many doors, none of them open. We sat and waited. As the day lengthened we continued to sit, cold, wet, and anxious, feeling totally out of control over our circumstances. Aware of a darkening mood, we stared at a fleet of army helicopters at the end of the field, mumbling assurances to each other. Suddenly one of the group, a lady of indeterminate age in a yellow rain slicker, jumped to her feet, jammed her hands in her pockets and began walking back and forth across in front of us, singing the cowboy song "Old Delores." The effect was immediate--the mood lifted as we became aware of a western folk singer named Katie Lee, now on stage in a deserted airfield in Kamchatka. It seemed possible that she had never played to a more appreciative audience.

As if on cue, the cloud bank began to roll back from the horizon, exposing a sliver of pale, creamy gray sky, a last gasp of the day. A whistle blew, we scrambled quickly to the aircraft, threw our gear in the cargo hold and ourselves into the chopper and as the rotors started turning, we lifted off. Twenty minutes later we landed in the Nalyichevo Valley, our trek begun.

A large vehicle, obviously our supply truck that resembled what the offspring of a tank and a semi might have looked like, dominated the scene. Scattered in the field nearby, little yellow tents bloomed like igloos. I lugged my duffle bag to one, claimed it mine, and crawled in, happy to be home. Spreading my ground cover, then a survival blanket, I unrolled my sleeping bag and offered a prayer that moisture wouldn't find me. Dampness surrounded us, the temperature was dropping, I was ready to hibernate.

A soft rain was falling the next morning as we hurried to the big six-tired, all-wheel-drive truck. Yuri, our driver, sat behind the wheel, ready to get started, a cigarette dangling from the corner of his mouth. He spoke no English, but his deeply lined face beamed a big smile as he fired up the engine, happy to ferry us to the starting point of our day's trek. The truck, built as a troop carrier for the military, was a behemoth able to traverse ice fields, swamps, rivers, mountains and uneven terrain, found its true calling in the days ahead. Questioning the design of the vehicle, we learned that the Soviets so feared an invasion of the peninsula, where a secret naval base was established, that they purposely did not build roads, making it difficult, if not impossible, for invaders to move troops about. Sobering to think that just two years earlier the seats we were sitting on were holding military in readiness to attack us. Now we rode in friendship.

Yuri drove until the road ended, then pointed the truck into the mountains. Up and up, in pouring rain and wind we climbed what must have been a ninety degree hillside, came to a relatively flat area and stopped. Our heart beats resumed a normal rhythm. This was our clue to get out and hike. In cold rain. Sanity was questioned, but ignored, after all, this is what we came for.

We slogged through mud, pulling our Gore-Tex rain gear closer as the wind picked up and rain pelted down in sharp bursts. Fog descended. One moment the jagged ridges of volcanos were visible, the next moment we passed a waterfall that tumbled into a cloud bank, the world a cottony void. We hiked on, found some hot springs, stopped to rest by the bit of warmth beside them, chewed on energy bars and took off again. Finally, summiting a peak, we sighted in the far distance below us, the yellow truck, our tents set up in the field, the mess tent ready to welcome us. Day one on the trail was about to come to a close. We'd done it!

The dining tent, set close beside the cooking tent, became our social hall. Coming into camp, we'd shed the outer layer of wet clothes we'd trekked in, then found comfort and companionship at a candle lit table, sharing tales of the day's adventure, sharing fellowship with these men and women who wanted to know so much about us, our country, our government. Most of the guides spoke some English, a subject taught in their schools, a fact that surprised most of us.

That first night, while peeling off wet clothing in the damp chill of my small tent, and pulling on thermal long johns, I crawled into my sleeping bag, making a promise to myself that I'd leave this part of the trip out of the tales I'd share with my husband. His idea of camping out was stopping at a Motel 6; the fact I'd spent time and money to hike in these cold, wet, conditions would be unfathomable to him. Some things are just better not shared. Or explained.

The pattern for the next few days had been established. Up early after a night's sound sleep, we downed a breakfast of juice, hot barley cereal, hearty bread and coffee --then Yuri would drive us to a drop off point and we'd begin the day's trek, or slog, it all depended on the weather. The tramps continued in cloudy, damp weather, not the hard rains of the first day, but just a foggy mist that sorta seeped into your pores, in spite of rain gear claims. We crossed fields where volcanos had tossed the earth's innards, basalt rocks that looked like black inked petrified sponges, some as big as boulders and some as small as pebbles, all hard to walk over. We learned to dance a "basalt two step" around and through them.

We trudged over fields of low plants that hugged the

thin soil. With their tiny red and gold blooms nestled among the green leaves, the scene reminded me of a gigantic oriental rug covering the landscape. Later the same day we trekked over black barren land, dotted with large patches of snow, or, as one fellow suggested later, maybe large patches of snow with black barren land around them. Whatever. I thought of a Holstein in my grandfather's herd and thirsted for a glass of milk.

Disappointed that a climb up the volcano Avachinsky had been forfeited when our plans were changed, we sighted a small volcano in the distance that seemed to be singing the song of the Lorelei. Four of us left our companions to trek on, shifted our back packs, and headed toward an ice field that lay between us and the summit.

With grit and determination in our bellies and grasping a hiking pole in each hand, we started across the glacier with our sights on Mt. Mutnovsky. Swathed in layers of silk, polypropylene, fleece and our waterproof shells, we were ready to take whatever the weather gods threw at us. We could have been welcomed in a Muslim neighborhood, nothing but our eyes visible as we pulled the drawstrings on our parkas tighter, covering our cheeks and forehead. Clouds continued to roll in, swirl around us, then lift. The wind picked up as light snow began to fall. We watched columns of vapor pour out of the crater, as we carefully picked our way across the ice.

After an hour or so of laboriously finding footholds, it became apparent that our boots were far from adequate for the challenge of the ice beneath our feet. Acknowledging the danger, we headed back to camp in a cold rain, back to where we knew there would be shelter and a warm fire, feeling much as I imagined our cave dwelling ancestors felt when approaching their cave-- something inborn, encoded there on our DNA over the millennium.

That night we gathered for our final evening around the table with our guides, Sergey, Sasha, Dimtry, Milhael and Natasha, not just guides anymore, we had bonded as friends. Sipping hot drinks, we laughed about our day's adventures, talked about our families, our lives, what we hoped the future would bring, now that Communism had fallen. It was a whole new world for all of us, who had been considered enemies, only a couple of years before.

Shortly after dawn the next morning, we packed our duffle bags, shouldered them, and ran through yet another downpour to climb aboard "Big Yellow," the giant all-terrain vehicle, ready for the next chapter of this topsy-turvy trip. Laughing, we remembered the lines in the trip description that claimed late August and early September were the optimum times to travel in Kamchatka, with warm sun, cool breezes, few bugs.

Maybe. Until a typhoon rages up the Pacific.

On our way to Petropavlovsk, we spent the night at a geologist's camp situated near hot springs. Time to luxuriate in a true Russian *banya* at the hot springs, a bath, sauna and then, digging through the duffle bag, finding dry, clean clothes. Refreshed and invigorated, we traveled on to the city for touristy fun, lunch, shopping and sightseeing, stopping first on a hillside overlooking the city and harbor. Replicas of Vitus Bering's ships, the St. Paul and St. Peter, the proud sailing vessels that brought him to this part of the world, had been erected on tall pedestals overlooking the bay. Its water was dotted that day with a fleet of vessels; sleek carriers, local fishing boats, huge tankers and cargo ships.

After a meal that featured squid in cream, we strolled around the streets, looking for shops that had caught on to the kitschy world of souvenirs for the tourist trade. A few tee shirts, with a belching volcano across the front and a back that announced to those behind you that: "KAMCHATKA IS A BEAUTIFUL PLACE, COME TO SEE IT WITH YOUR OWN EYES," were in the cases and shelves, along with obligatory ashtrays and paper weights.

We marveled at the number of book and map stores along the wide boulevard. Standing in front of a map display in a small shop, I became aware of the bold placement of the Soviet Union, Europe, Africa and Australia, front and center, while North and South America were shuttled off to the left of the map. So different from the maps I'd lived with, with the Americas holding prime position. I brought that map home with me, and it still hangs on my wall as a reminder of world perspective, that the United States is not the center of the universe.

With Yuri at the wheel of Big Yellow we took off in late afternoon for the Bystraya River, the massive truck lurching through boreal forests of birch, poplar and larch as night closed in. Suddenly we made a turn in the road and there before us in the headlights, we sighted the river, then our boats and guides.

Yellow tents blossomed in a circle around the camp fire and a makeshift shelter that would serve as our dining tent. Those ingenious hunters and fishermen who had offered to shepherd us on short notice, had erected two of the large river rafts on end, stretched and tethered a large sheet of plastic across them. The men stood there, smiling their welcome and offering calloused hands to help us.

After hurriedly stowing our duffle bags in tents and running back through wet grass in the misty twilight, we huddled under the plastic make-do roof. A big pot of fish chowder hung above a blazing fire on a makeshift arm of wood. We filled our bowls with chowder, replete with fresh fish, potatoes, onions, and fragrant with fresh dill, picked up slices of thick black bread, settled back to enjoy the meal. We decided we'd never eaten better.

Though unspoken, the question "Will this weather pattern change?" seemed to permeate the air around us as we made our way back to our tents for the night. Determined to think positively and to make the best of whatever fell, we were grateful for those cups of hot soup that soothed our tired souls and a dry spot in a sodden land to collect our thoughts.   .

We awoke to a low cloud cover and a hint that sun might break through. Had the gods we importuned the night before heard us? After hurrying through a breakfast of hot porridge, stout biscuits, honey and strong coffee, we packed our gear in dry bags, stored them in the rafts and launched into the river, spirits high, hearts light.

Our orange riverboats were surplus military pontoon rafts, each holding four persons, two guides and two tourists. Among the guides were men who had been members of the Soviet Navy submarine crews, smiling, strong, happy-go-lucky guys who were proud of their little flotilla. I wondered aloud one day, "How does it feel to be paddling down a river on a little raft after being fathoms deep under an ocean in a submarine?" The translator posed the question to the oarsmen; one thought a moment and replied, "Is better here, I can see the sky."

The river was mighty and wide, with crystal clear water allowing us to peer down to the rock strewn bed, a river with large gravel bars, areas of riffles that we'd barely slide over, with only one small rapid to run. Slowly, languorously, the guides would dip their paddles into the river, give a little pull, then drift with the current. A few times we'd lash rafts together and just float, maybe offer a few observations, but for the most part we sat in silent reverie, letting the experience, the magnificence of the wilderness in this untouched land, soak into our souls.

We floated along for a few days, under mostly cloudy skies, though occasionally we enjoyed a sun break. In those moments when the sun would shine, the intensity of light turned the water a deep blue, the choppy little white caps shone brighter, and the world turned crystal clear. In view of a mountain range, we slid silently past huge granite outcroppings covered in thick vegetation that jutted into the water's edge much like the Dells of Wisconsin, past forests that ended where the rock strewn beach began.

Several times a day we'd pull onto a beach, a time to stretch our legs, to hike into the woods or grasslands, or to stroll the rocky shore. If we neared a meadow, we'd search for blueberry thickets, hoping to fill our caps or zip lock bags with the berries and carry them back to chef Irina. We'd be rewarded for our efforts with Mopc, a hot blueberry drink, a honeyed nectar the gods would've approved of. On other breaks, we ventured short distances into the dense, rainforest-like vegetation, Pushing through tall grasses, some that grew head high, I came to know a plant with long blade-shaped leaves whose serrated edges left a sharp cut on skin that brushed against them. Guides, who kept a visual contact on our whereabouts, called it bear grass.

As we walked along the shoreline and back into the undergrowth, we kept a sharp eye out for signs of the legendary Kamchatka Brown Bear, a force of nature that sometimes weighs over fourteen hundred pounds, with paw prints that are easily discernible, some leaving an imprint of over twenty inches. I hoped we'd never see one . . . then again, a photo of my foot print next to the bear's would be a trophy.

At the first sighting of a bear ambling along the shore, my
heart skittered to an unfamiliar beat as the giant paused,
leveled his head and stared at the boats, and maybe what
could be white meat for dinner. There was no way I wanted
to see *Ursus Arctos Beringianus* or even a paw print up
close.

Lazing along the river, binoculars in hand, the two
birders of the group enjoyed field days as they found and
added new birds to their life lists. The rest of us would nod
approvingly as they exclaimed over a new find, but not
until we rounded a bend in the river and sighted a Steller's
Sea Eagle, did the non-birders snap to full attention.

A large bird (some weight up to 20 pounds), it perched
majestically on the top branches of a larch tree, a short way
off the river. The guides stilled their paddles, and we
silently drifted closer and closer . . . then it suddenly lifted
itself into the sky on ever widening circles, lazily drifting

higher and higher till it became a black speck. Perhaps to float on air currents until it found another promising tree branch near the river, one where it could leisurely regard its next meal, the fish mass below.

Since childhood I'd known that "salmon go home to spawn." I read it, saw pictures of their migration, listened to stories about it, but nothing could have prepared me for the sight of a river thick with salmon.

Leaving the rafts in the shallows we picked our way to the beach through a mass of writhing, thrashing salmon headed upstream. After two to five years in the Sea of Okhotsk, they'd begun their odyssey to their birthplace, in the high reaches of the region, by swimming first up the Bolshaya River, then the Byastrya to spawn. Directed home by what? A sense of light or smell, a magnetic pull? They swam, climbed, hurtled themselves up river in a frantic effort to get to the place they found life, losing weight, scales, and their color. The fish beneath our feet bore testament to that. Many were faded to a dull grey-shaded pale orange, their beauty lost on their frenzied mission to complete the journey home.

Our Russian hosts soon became more than kindly faces with unfamiliar names. as their personalities began to emerge; one was a dreamer, two were serious and studious, others jokers, always smiling and laughing among themselves. Dressed in camouflage, a macho man wowed onlookers as he shaved with his hunting knife, no mirror, his eyes turned to the sky as he wielded the blade across his face. It was rumored there were KGB agents among the guides, put on the trip to "observe things." Whether or not this was true, all proved earnest in their attention to the river and our welfare.

One afternoon, Irina, the thoughtful lone woman among the Russian guides, the one who oversaw the feeding and nourishment of the group, joined us for a walk in the woods. With eyes twinkling, she suddenly held up her arm, (the international stop signal) stopped and broke a piece of a tall plant with a hollow, pipe like stem. Smiling a pixie like smile, perhaps remembering a childhood memory, she unsheathed her knife, peeled off the bark, drilled holes in the stem, put it to her lips and played a flute melody. The Pan of Kamchatka.

Those rugged country folk saw to it that we ate well as we floated along the river, with foods as sturdy and hearty as the crew that guided us. Meals were served on a blue and white checked oil cloth, spread wherever we happened to be, on a rocky shore, a sandy beach or grassy meadow. Our breakfasts consisted of hot porridge, jam and bread, our lunches dark bread, sausage and cheese. All meals were served with mugs of hot, strong tea.

Fish was a staple of our evening meals. Sometimes, during the day floats the guides would put their paddles down and reach for their fly rods to cast for rainbow trout. Farther down river we ate salmon, baked in leaves, roasted on a spit, or chopped in a rich chowder. Beets, cucumbers, potatoes and carrots appeared on our plates in surprisingly original guises.

Bugs seemed nonexistent as we floated on the river, usually in a good, stiff breeze. It was another story when we put ashore in late afternoon and set up camp. Doused with Deet or other bug repellant, most of the group found it necessary to don the mosquito net veiled hats we'd been advised to pack, but a few just batted at the little black no-see-ums or sat in the downwind of the campfire smoke. The little critters were everywhere, in our eyes, ears, noses, hair, and occasionally we swallowed them.

One evening as dinner was called, we were handed cups of hot soup to begin the meal. One of the guests, a firebrand of a woman who had a history of telling it like it was, sat staring into her cup, looking at a host of tiny black bugs that had landed on the creamy broth. After a moment or two, she lifted the mosquito netting that covered her face, said "All right you little sons-of-bitches, down the hatch," put the cup to her lips and drained it. Satisfied, she flashed a smile as she lowered her cup. Our protein came in many guises.

On a more memorable evening, while digging through the raft that held provisions, Irina announced, "No fish or bugs tonight," and pulled from provisions a large, pale green glass jar filled with sauerkraut. Simmered with sausage and potatoes, it was a dish to delight any Northern European.

Covetously, I eyed the empty jar and asked if I could have it. The guides passed puzzled glances among themselves, "a sauerkraut jar?" With a shrug and an "of course" nod, it was handed to me. I wrapped it well in clothing and it went into my dry bag for the river trip, then eventually into my carry-on for the long flight home.

That jar is in my kitchen today, sitting on a ledge that catches the early light of the day. Some mornings, just glancing at its green translucence, speckled with imperfections of tiny air bubbles, I'm back floating on the Bystraya. And wondering, again, how I could have been so lucky.

All too soon, we began our journey home. As we drifted around a bend in the river, we sighted Yuri and "Big Yellow" waiting on the bank near a bridge. The oarsmen paddled faster; we pulled in and began unloading our rafts. The time had come to pack up our gear and memories, time to say "*Dasveedahnya,*" a Russian good-bye.

But before we left the river adventures and the guides who'd made them possible, we participated in farewell ceremonies. The first, was a traditional dunking for guides completing their first trip down river. Lovely initiate Irina just shrugged, smiled and prepared to take the ceremony in stride. One guide held her under the arms, another lifted her feet, a quick dip, then clapping and cheers and it was over. Laughing, she adjusted her red cap and rejoined the group.

Then one by one, our names were called, and certificates of achievement were given to us. Mine reads, "To Aleen Steinberg, from Florida, on raft #2, led by Alexander, by the decision of the Administration ULCYU (Leninist Communism Youth Union) and by the committee of the tourist Club ViLui for the participation in rafting Bystraya River on 7 September 1993 having taken 1st place." Today it hangs beside a map of Kamchatka on my office wall.

After a few tears, many heartfelt thanks, hugs, and a host of "we'll never forget you's," we said good-bye to the crew, and climbed aboard Big Yellow, bound back to Petropavlovsk.

Weary, in need of hot baths and a good night's sleep in a bed, we stopped again at the geologist's camp in Yelizovo, just outside the city. It was still the same long two story building, white paint chipped and peeling, but after days sleeping in small tents in wet grass or on beaches near the river, we now saw the camp as a grand hotel. Room to stand while changing clothes, running water, beds with legs, all spelled comfort and civilization.

The next morning, with hours to ourselves before the scheduled late afternoon departure, a couple of us took advantage of the time to wander through the streets and neighborhoods. There were a few log houses, the rest were made of roughhewn lumber. The carpenters who built these took obvious pride in their creations; each house possessed some distinctive woodwork, either on the doors or around the windows. Many were framed with colorful peasant or folk art designs, similar to those found in Scandinavia. Picket fences surrounded the houses, vegetable and flower gardens flourished behind them, and here and there greenhouses took advantage of the geothermal activity burbling beneath the ground.

We happened by a house with large flower beds, where late blooming zinnias, marigolds and asters grew beside yellow roses climbing a trellis. Two women, sisters we learned later, came out of the house to say "hello," share their garden, and offer us what turned out to be an unforgettable interlude, a visit in their home.

They spoke no English, and we understood only few words of Russian, but we managed to communicate through our eyes, gestures and smiles, along with the help of a Lonely Planet vocabulary book, ever present in my back pack. They asked us in for *chai*, or tea.

We entered a small, cozy room; one wall was draped with a colorful paisley shawl, and on another wall hung a large velvet throw, its background of deep yellow and black tiger stripes was centered with a painting of a large Siberian tiger's head. The Russians take great pride in those giants of the Amur region, far to the north.

Scurrying about, determined to help us feel comfortable, they directed us to a small couch and a couple of chairs, one sister fluffing and straightening pillows. They opened cupboards and brought out treasures of canned ham, biscuits, and crackers. It took a few minutes to convince them we weren't hungry, so we finally settled on tea and sweets. Sipping, smiling, and gesturing, we had just settled down, when one of the sisters jumped up and went to a little screened porch, returning with a bucket in her hand and smile on her face.

Hand-painted red, yellow and blue flowers adorned the side of the white enamel bucket that held close to five gallons of blueberries. It was set on the floor before us, and we were each handed a spoon and given the order "*Naslazhdaytes*" or enjoy.

That command still rings true as I relive those days in Kamchatka. Enjoy! In spite of the hardships of a well-planned adventure that began with an 180° turn that could have put our entire trip at risk, only the happy memories remain. We enjoyed!

Keepin' On, Walkin' On

Chapter 5

Artic

BIRTH OF A TERRITORY UNDER A BLUE MOON
MARCH 31, 1999

Under a full moon and braving forty below wind chill,
I stood with a parka- clad crowd gathered on the shore of
Frobisher Bay, watching as fireworks exploded into huge
chrysanthemums of green, orange, red and yellow petals
that burst and streamed toward the frozen earth. How
propitious, that second full moon of the month, helping
signal at midnight the birth of Nunavut, a new Territory in
the high Arctic, a territory one-fifth of Canada's land mass,
730,000 square miles with one paved road and 25,000
people.

The Birth of a Territory. In the bone chilling, numbing
cold I wrapped my arms around myself and my mind

around the night, listening as the crowds cheered and shouted in jubilation as the fireworks lit the sky, then tumbled in comets of color toward land. The joy of the people was palpable, a bold initiative to restore land to an aboriginal people. The new nation called Nunavut, "*Our Land*" in the Inuit language, Inuktitut, was about to come true. I thought about their years of struggles, of how they had hoped, waited, and worked toward these moments. Now the formation of a new government, their government, with a native Parliament was about to come true. With a sudden rush, the privilege of being there and having the opportunity of sharing this moment with people I'd come to know and care for, struck me with a force I hadn't reckoned with. It was the kind of moment you never want to forget, the kind you tuck away in your heart and hold as precious and powerful.

I thought about my journey to this celebration. From Ottawa to Iqaluit, the day before had been one of stark contrasts. Leaving the capital city of Canada, I'd driven past elegant, stately old world Parliament Buildings, the Canadian government's monuments to man's law and order, and flown to the Arctic; I'd walked to a high school gym where I watched a new government sworn in. From a city of paved streets and sidewalks to a hamlet with dirt roads and polar bear skins stretched on frames to dry in side yards, from rubbing shoulders with mink coats and Brooks Brothers suits to embracing friends whose parkas and leggings were made of reindeer, seal, and polar bear skins.

The plane from Ottawa to Iqaluit had been packed with journalists, camera and TV crews, media reps, bureaucrats, and tourists, in what could best be described as "we're on our way to watch something wonderful happen." It was a festive, holiday, feel-good mood that would last throughout the two days of celebration. My seat mate, a reporter from Ireland, asked what prompted me to make this journey; I satisfied her question with "A lifelong interest in these native peoples." Then I let my mind drift back to an obscure article in the *Tampa Tribune*, in the spring of '82, when the Northwest Territory voted to divide itself and create Nunavut. It was one of those little one or two liners under a NEWS OF CANADA column that many papers carry.

It was a spring morning. I was barefoot as I carried the paper into the house; I couldn't remember much about the article, only that it grabbed my attention. I remember thinking, "at last, justice for a proud people who had the word Eskimo thrown at them by the whites centuries ago." Long a champion of human rights, stories like that had significant meaning for me . . . and the meaning stayed with me.

Under the light of the fireworks my mind backspaced to the winter of ''97, when I spent a week traveling in the high Arctic with two guides, their dog teams and sleds, where the after-dinner conversation, whether in an igloo or snow tent, often turned to the promise of their own land and self-government. The seed was sown. I would return to witness history made.

In early winter of '99 I contacted an outfitter to arrange the trip to the new Territory. Weeks went by, and my plans were finalized, only to be canceled. "No room at the inn." In the new capital Iqaluit, a town of 4,500 with 140 hotel rooms for an expected influx of 800, the sold-out sign was posted. My heart sank, I'd have to miss this chance of a lifetime. Ah, but thanks to the ingenuity of some local entrepreneurs, beds were found, in private residences, military barracks, and school classrooms. I lucked out, being housed at the home of the Wildlife Resource Officer and his family; my seat mate was issued a cot at the local drug and alcohol treatment center, where many of the media were housed.

After I'd met and checked in with my host family, I slipped and slid back to the dirt road that doubled as the main street of Iqaluit. There were many new improvements to the town since my last visit; my destination, the Parnaivik Building, headquarters for the games, races, exhibits, and competition was one of them, paved roads were not.

Outside, were net races, between long lengths of fish net that had been stretched out. Two participants crawled under one end, then raced on hands and knees to the other end. Mittens flew off as they crawled over the ice, twisted and tangled in the net till the end was reached. I watched men toss harpoons at a block of ice instead of a seal, and a four men strap pull, each pulling in each direction till one overcame the others.

The mercury stood at -13°. Reaching the numb stage, I went inside to watch the whalebone carvers, then to the stage area to watch a troupe of Reindeer Dancers.. The obvious leader of the group of students moved like a Baryshnikov, another beat a drum with powerful intensity and passion. Thawed, I returned to the main center where crates of frozen chunks of char were piled around. Folks walking by picked up a piece and nibbled on it as we would an apple. Before long a huge blue plastic drop cloth was spread out on the ground, and boxes and cases of frozen fish and caribou were emptied upon it. As the crowd gathered, people were given plastic bags, then all stood quietly, hats off and heads bowed, as an Elder gave thanks to the land and the sea for the bounty before them. A whistle sounded and the race was on to fill their bags with as much food as they could.

The swearing in of the Commissioner of Nunavut took place in the Inuksuk high school's gym, its walls covered with art depicting the Inuit's struggle to attain self - government.

The Commissioner was sworn in first, a small woman with a kindly face and a sad, gentle smile. She was sworn in three languages, French, English and Inuktitut, then responded in English and Inuktitut. As she recalled the struggle of the past twenty years she recounted the efforts of her husband who had died in April, one year to the day before this dream would come true. Breaking down, she cried unabashedly. There weren't many dry eyes in the room as her daughter, then son and extended family came to console her.

The Premier, Paul Okalik, a young man of 34, was sworn in next. It was quite a month for this man, the first Inuit to obtain a law degree. He overcame teen age drinking problems, and the grief surrounding the suicide of a brother. In the last thirty days his accomplishments had included passing the Bar, being elected to the Legislative Assembly and being elected Premier.

After going through the receiving line, I returned home to find the house full, a crowd of teen-agers in the kitchen and a host of adults in the living room, all with bowls of caribou stew. I joined them, with a hunk of bannock and my bowl of stew, to swap stories and impressions of the day. Sitting there, I glanced up at a TV screen and watched a replay of the ceremonies that had taken place a couple hours earlier play out, and suddenly saw myself, my bright red jacket standing out in the audience. Then, glancing out to the kitchen, my gaze fell on several women and children gathered around a large piece of a cardboard box, flattened on the floor, eating frozen arctic char that they thinly sliced off the whole fish. I thought, what dichotomy, the technology to watch myself as I was hours earlier next to people savoring a delicacy in a manner that probably hasn't changed in hundreds of years . . . except now they had cardboard to spread before them.

Excusing myself from the celebration, I said "good night" to the revelers and headed to my room for a welcome rest. It had been a long day, filled with powerful moments, and I was exhausted.

But sleep eluded me. My mind began to drift over the day and then like a magic lantern show, it was swept away with memories of that first trip to Baffin Island in '97, and a week dogsledding with three Inuits as guides and companions. It was a personal and profoundly moving adventure in a harsh, but beautiful land. There was a fragility to the days there, where there are a hundred words for snow.

My mind wandered on, remembering. The seeds for that adventure were probably sown when, on my sixth birthday, my parents gave me a book about the Laplanders, or caribou hunters of the high Arctic countries. Fifty years later on a trip across Siberia, I met a Laplander serving as a crew member on the Lake Baikal expedition. Listening to the interpreter recount his stories of herding reindeer and living in the freezing and unforgiving lands of the far North, I was convinced that a trip there was my goal. My lifelong fascination with people who make do with so little to work with, would become a reality.

And a few years later it did. With months of preparation under my belt, I was on my way to Baffin Island. Funny how a little thing convinced me my dream was about to come true . . . driving to the airport I had glanced down at my hands on the wheel and noted there was no wide gold band on my left hand. That ring had been with me for forty eight years. and I felt naked staring at the mark it left on my finger. But it had to be, I'd been advised not to wear any rings, because they would only conduct cold to my hands.

Images of the days that followed flashed across my mind's eye. We had traveled in two sleds with twenty-two dogs, the drivers and my guide, existing in many respects as they had for centuries. The isolation of living with them in a snow tent or igloo offered a chance for unforgettable cross-cultural exchanges and more than a fair share of memorable moments. There was much to get used to: the rhythm of the sled, the gait of the dogs, the sight of them as they fanned out in in their leads streaking across the frozen tundra. The dogs would go wild when they saw the drivers coming in the morning. Born to run and haul a sled, they were in their element, barking and dancing around as they were hitched up. On the first day we traveled in a hard snow storm for the first few hours, and the wind blew what felt like stinging icy shards of glass into my face. I tightened the hood of the parka around my face, peering out at a world framed in beautiful dark, brown fur. What, I wondered, mink, marten, sable? Maybe just dark summer caribou.

Nope, I learned later it was dog. Like every other animal in the Arctic, nothing of them is wasted.

Clothed in caribou skins and listening to the sound of the sled runners as we were carried across the ice fields, I became aware of an almost holy connection to the past and future, as though all time were now. Touched by something deep and archetypal, I experienced a sense of peace, of being at one with the universe.

But of all the treasured memories of that Arctic adventure, none was as special and unforgettable as the hours spent in a whiteout.

On a morning toward the end of our trip, as we dismantled camp and packed the sleds, light snow began to fall. We had spent the night on an inland lake and the route to land over the ice was a hard pull for the dogs, so I walked beside them for most of the first hour. Reaching the blue ice of the Foxe Basin, I had just settled into the sled when snow began to come down harder. Suddenly it was everywhere. Not really flakes but a snow dust, powder, vapor, fog, cloud. I couldn't find a word for it. I was simply encased in soft, feathery, whiteness.

Snuggling under the reindeer skins, we rode for hours in a world without dimension, no land, no sky, no horizon. Just an eternity of white nothingness. Linear time disappeared as the dogs pulled on and suddenly my place in the overall scheme of things became quite clear, I was but a speck in a cloud on this planet Earth.

Now, years later I smile as I recount my delight and wonder in the frozen world that my friends find so alien. I smile because I think I know why that book on Laplanders touched a six year old so profoundly. DNA research done on my cheek swab by National Geographic's Human Genome Study revealed that 12,000-15,000 years ago my ancestors roamed Northern Europe and were known as the Saami, the Reindeer people.

I was at one with the Inuit.

The day of the BIRTH OF A TERRITORY April 1, 1999, dawned bright and cold.

I answered the cab driver's "where to?" with, "To the FOL Hangers," and settled back, catching my breath after a run from the house in forty below wind chill. How appropriate, I thought, to the FOL hangers. During the Second World War, the U.S. Air Force, with the blessing of the Canadian Government, had selected the land around what is now known as the town of Iqaluit, to build an airstrip, long enough to handle large aircraft transporting war materials from the United States to European allies. These huge hangers. Forward Operation Landing, built for war, were now finding use in peace to launch a new nation.

As I stepped out of the cab, the driver wished me "good day and good luck," then added "Lady, there is no way you're going to get into this hanger, it's been reserved for weeks for dignitaries."

I thanked him for the ride, his good wishes and counsel, took a deep breath, and strode into the hanger.

Gathering courage I approached the officer seated at the reception desk and said "Aleen Steinberg, Tampa Florida, requesting special guest pass." He glanced up at me, said "You've come along way, haven't you?" I smiled and answered, "So have the Inuits." He handed me the pass. OH-MY-GOD, I was in.

There were 400 seats in the cavernous hanger, Royal Mounted Police in their spit and polish uniforms were stationed in front of walls covered in room size canvases of native art. Inukshuks, igloos, land animals, sea creatures, arctic flowers, and hundreds of hand prints of the children that had fashioned the designs, offered a sense of place under the ceiling's steel beams. I glanced back at the area where the dignitaries were gathering for their procession to their places of honor. The Prime Minister of Canada; the Governor General; the Secretary of Indian Affairs in their pinstripes and polished shoes, Behind them came the new officers of Nunavut in reindeer vests and sealskin *kamiks.*

The room filled quickly with young and old, some in clothing from a mall or a mail order, some in native dress. Lavishly embroidered flowers of the tundra adorned many of the women's parkas; some carried sleeping babies nestled in their *amuntis*, the large hoods of their parkas.

The hour struck, the room was pitched into blackness and suddenly the stage became a muted symphony of dancing lights; turquoise, amber, purple, blue flashing and streaming down as they do in the northern skies. Onstage the dances began, first the drum dancers, each beat pounding on the senses in exhalation, as if to say, "Nunavut has come to be." Then the joyous reindeer dancers, bucking and bending across the stage as if in play on a north field in awakening spring. Finally, the deep tones of throat singers vibrating, carrying sounds that I imagined might have sounded like those from the center of the Earth. In the time of Creation.

The lights went on again and elders lit the *Qulliq*, the traditional seal oil lamp signifying the hearth and warmth of a home. A story teller wove a tale of the land and culture of pre-contact times, the appearance of white men, land negotiations, and the Birth of Nunavut.

The Commitment Ceremony began. The Premier stood and said "We have come to recognize the right of the people of the North to take control of their destiny." The room fell quiet. I glanced at the faces around me: proud, some passive, some smiling, many with tears running down their cheeks. My heart became full, full of admiration for the Inuit who worked so tirelessly for their independence and had seen this day come true, and full of gratitude for the chance to witness this day-The Birth of a Territory.

Then as drums rolled a steady beat, the Flag was unfurled for the first time. There it was, the Inuit's own. The room exploded in joy and applause, whistles, and laughter bounced off the walls and made a music all its own.

The flag with a yellow and white background symbolizing the land, snow and sunshine, in the center an Inuksuk, a stone monument that serves to guide people on land, and finally, in the upper right hand corner, a North Star, traditional guide for navigation, forever remaining unchanged. As dependable as the wisdom of a community's elders.

TO THE HIGH NORTH

Having moved from the large hangers to the airport, parts of last night's gala celebration were still rocking on in full melody the next morning. Local celebs, guitars, fiddles, TV crews, press, old friends and new faces seemed determined to prolong this new day of independence; it was not to fade away quietly. Nor was it to fade from my mind. As I made my way to the end of the runway where the small plane and bush pilot waited to carry me to the high north, I looked back and saw a small group, arms entwined, stomping and singing as a Inuit troubadour walked with them strumming his guitar.

The flight toward the Circle over mountains and sheer cliffs of ice was dazzling in the morning sun, I thrilled at the crystal world below and wondered at the promise of adventure in those snowy lands. Landing, the Bush pilot dropped me, my gear, and a sack of mail at a small airstrip outside the outpost town of Keykicktacjoac, then radioed the guide that we'd landed, assured me the guide would be there shortly, and flew off. I stood waiting in the small wooden shack. Moments later, Steve, the man who was to be my guide on this trip above the Arctic Circle, roared up on a skidoo. He appeared to be a man of few words as he fastened my duffle bag to a rack, told me to climb behind him and hang on. I did, and we took off like we were jet propelled, no easy pedal. He floored it and we flew.

We were scheduled to leave that afternoon, but our provisions were still in Montreal and until they came, we weren't budging. So . . . time for a briefing in the small room that served as the guest house coffee shop. His comments were brief and to the point. "Though my name is Steve, you will call me by my Inuit name, Kisak. You will learn Inuit on this trip. I can travel with just one sled and a woman, but I want another guide for safety reasons." I breathed a sigh of relief. His eyes firmed up and he spoke slowly and deliberately "Polar bears are a constant danger, I sleep with a gun by my side. Don't ever leave the tent or igloo without me."

I replied, "O.K. Kisak."

Again "Don't ever leave the shelter unless I'm with you."

"I understand, Kisak."

Then, after a long pause, he slapped his hand flat on the table and said, "Not even if you have to pee." Satisfied that he'd made his point he went on "if our food doesn't come, we'll have to stock up at the Northern Store." Knowing how the guides pride themselves with being able to offer their clients treats from the mainland, I could sense his disappointment, and assured him that noodles, char and chocolate would do me just fine for the week we'd be out. He checked my eyes for honesty, smiled, we loaded up. On the sled, I cocooned myself in reindeer skins, and the two of us were off in a bitter cold wind. The dogs, born to run, yipped, yelped, and skimmed over the ice for a couple hours, happy to be in harness again.

Suddenly, and abruptly, Kisak pulled the dogs to a halt, climbed off the sled, and announced, "We stop here." While I danced around trying to keep warm, he put the snow tent up, started a small stove, and set about cutting ice blocks to position around the bottom sides of the tent. As Northern lights danced against the jagged cliffs of ice, another team and guide roared up. The man I came to know as "gentle David" got out, threw a smile my way, picked up an axe, and began cutting ice.

As the weak sunlight faded, the guys hustled to secure the tent, then set about building a snow shelf to hold our sleeping bags. I watched, fascinated, as they fashioned the shelf, about 2 feet high, out of hard packed snow in the rear of the tent, then spread reindeer skins, our sleeping bags, then another reindeer skin. That night, cocooned in my sleeping bag, with another reindeer skin thrown over me, and sandwiched between Kisak and David in their covers, I drifted off to sleep wishing I had a snapshot of this Arctic "*ménage a trios*."

I awoke to an Easter Sunday to remember. The tent was frigid as I crawled out of my warm cocoon and began layering yet more clothing on top of silk, dammar, EC2 shell and sweater that I'd slept in, in order to visit the snow latrine. (Those necessary visits fell into a quickly understood routine between us: because of the danger of bears, lookouts were necessary. As there were no bushes on that frozen tundra to slip behind, we'd request a moment of privacy, then the other two would turn their backs. When finished an O.K. was sounded and we'd be back in the igloo or tent or on the trail.) All told that morning, by the time I'd gotten to my baklava, hat, goggles and mittens I had twenty one items of clothing on my body.

Outside a hard wind whipped the tent and as thick snow pelted down, a cloud of deep gloom descended in the tent. As we ate our breakfast of oatmeal with brown sugar in silence, I wondered what kind of calculations were making tracks in Kisak's brain. There was a lot to be considered if we were snowed in for a day or two. But suddenly, Joy! The wind abruptly died down, the blinding snow became a sprinkling, and gloom lifted as quickly as it had set in. The order to "pack it up and move it out" was issued.

The men moved like a precision drill team, the sleds were packed in short order, the dogs harnessed and we were off toward icebergs on the far horizon. With good sledding for the first hour or so, our sleds flew across the ice; then the day's trip began to morph into a hard one, as we hit soft snow that had drifted into slanted ice cards, stacked haphazardly across the horizon. Kisak, having a hard time managing the sled across the drifts, finally got off the sled and helped the dogs pull. Then, as the wind picked up a whiteout blew in, the trail disappeared and we called it quits early; no igloo tonight, just get the tent up and get inside, chop, chop.

As I watched the two quickly set up camp . . . here the stove, there the food box, in back the skins and sleeping bags, in front of the tent our few personal belongings, then out to care for the dogs, not a movement was wasted. Being in their intense, high charged energy field was like being plugged into high voltage, but I needed all the energy I could muster just to shed my boots and outer layers.

After the small stove was lit, It took only a few minutes for the tent to warm up enough to relax and have a cup of tea. A lazy afternoon stretched in front of me, with not much chance for a lot of conversation because David spoke little English and Kisak was wrapped in his own thoughts. Remembering whiteouts from a previous Arctic trip, I'd brought a book, a sketch pad, and a deck of cards to while away time in case of delays, now the moment seemed a good one for a game of solitaire. As I pulled out the cards and shuffled them, David/'s face lit up and he said "Cribbage?"

I repeated, rather incredulously, "Cribbage?" He beamed and shook his head "Yes." Cribbage was a game I'd learned as a child, the unofficial card game of the large German population in my Wisconsin's home town. But how did it get to the Inuits? Kisak explained that the men from Northern Europe, who had come to the Arctic in the '50's during the Cold War to build the Distant Early Warning (DEW) Line, had brought their cribbage boards. During snowstorms and the long winter nights the Inuits had watched the men peg their games and had become quick and skillful students.

So, without benefit of a pegging board, but armed with paper and pencil to keep score, we began the first of many intense, hard fought games over the next week. Slowly, the language barrier between David and myself broke down. We began our communication with the "fifteen-twos" of the game invented, improved, codified more than three hundred years ago by Sir John Suckling, a young English poet and soldier.

That night, I was on the verge of falling into deep slumber, when low rumblings and growls began outside among the dogs. Kisak shot out of his sleeping bag in a flash with his 303 Winchester rifle in hand, David behind him. They quickly pulled on their snow gear, parkas and boots, then issued the warning, "Polar bear, stay in the tent." As if I needed to be told.

Maybe twenty minutes later the dogs quieted down, the men returned to the tent, flashlights were extinguished, sleeping bags were re-zipped and the silence was broken only by soft snores. I found sleep impossible and lay there letting thoughts and images race across my mind like the northern lights that had been dancing across the heavens earlier.

How in the name of all that's holy had I ended up in a snow tent, above the Arctic Circle, with a wind chill -40 outside, zipped in a sleeping bag, buried under reindeer skins, sandwiched between two Inuits and considering the actions of a polar bear within shouting distance. The god Hypnos finally claimed me and I slept.

I learned to understand the why's and the rhythm of David's whistled tune each morning as he stood watching a pan of simmering cereal. Every time a bubble of porridge burbled up he'd change the pitch or intensity of the whistle, slowly at first, followed by quick whistles of a merry tune of high and low notes as the bubbles broke the surface with soft puffs.

But understanding eluded me when I watched his early morning ritual. Leaving the sleeping shelf he'd kneel near the opening of the tent or igloo, extending his arms full length at each side, palms up. His eyes then turned down to his right hand as he ever so slowly arched his face to the ceiling and then down to his left hand on an imaginary arc, all the while chanting slowly and softly.

On the third morning curiosity got the better of me, and I asked. Kisak explained, "He is thanking his Creator for the gift of today, and asking help to follow its light till days end for the gift of life that is in it." My heart caught, I understood and felt a sudden kinship to this man. For back home, in a frame by the right side of my bathroom mirror, was a copy of the "*Salutation to the Dawn*" translated from the Sanskrit. It begins; "Look to this day for it is life, the very life of life" . . . I'd voiced that prayer every morning for years, reading those lines, asking my Creator to bestow the same grace, as the man kneeling was asking.

That morning a hard wind raged outside the tent as a storm blew in, whipping and drifting snow with a sudden fury. Our gear was packed ready to be loaded onto the sleds, but we could do nothing but sit and wait, anxious to go. Kisak sat in deep contemplative thought, his fingers drumming on his knee, he finally looked up, shrugged his shoulders and said, "The river runs the show." I looked at him; he smiled, shrugged his shoulders again and observed, "Blizzards don't care about odysseys."

Kisak, a forceful pragmatist . . . David, dreamer and poet.

The wind kept blowing; the morning moved on. Maybe we'd leave today, maybe we wouldn't. After the intense pace of past few days, killing time presented a new challenge. We began to share our lives, our other worlds. Mine was the first to be examined. What was my house like? My children and grandchildren? Did I have a dog, what kind, and what did it do? What food did I like to eat, and the weather? Land down below in the States, indeed the world, was no mystery to these Inuits who had access to the Discovery Channel in their villages. Florida? A land of sunshine, warm beaches, the Everglades, palm trees and flowers. David's face lit up at the idea of such a land. For fun I asked what he would do if he lived in such a world. His eyes locked onto a land far away. He considered my question for a few moments then answered "I would run across the sand and into the water and I'd just swim and swim with water all over me."

"With water all over me." Had he never experienced it? I'll probably never swim again without remembering that phrase.

By late morning the storm had spent itself, we quickly loaded the sleds and left with GPS in hand, trying to find the trail. Once it was located, the dogs, glad to be in harness, flew across the Arctic ice sheet. Suddenly, we sighted icebergs. There stood Gibraltar, beyond it the Sydney Opera house, there a castle on the Rhine and here a Quonset hut. Nearly incomprehensible in their size, the giants loomed above the flat snow fields with a powerful majesty, an unknown hand's sculptures.

With no floe edge in sight, we headed for further icebergs to climb and sight, taking time out for our daily refueling treats. First a frozen Arctic Char met the ax, its small pieces tasty and rich, laughingly referred to as Arctic Ice Cream. Our little butane stove was lit; ice melted and boiled for noodles in a cup, then hot cocoa. Re-energized we were off to the top of the next iceberg. There, after scowling, and much scanning of the horizon, the guys' grins broke out. The floe edge was sighted! On the lookout now for seals, whales and polar bears-we skimmed over the ice. Then far away on the sky line- a polar bear sighting.

We flew for about half hour behind a couple dogs that had been let out of harness, caught up to them, and within a respectable safe distance of the Arctic Bear, got off the sled. There it stood, against the late afternoon light, a massive, creamy, seven feet, maybe 1500 pounds of muscled lightning, black nose and eyes pointed at us, watching us, ready to move, considering its options.

In the raw presence of this wild animal, my heart thumped, adrenaline rushed, and I thrilled at how lucky I was to be in its presence.

Then I suddenly wished I hadn't intruded into its world.

Chapter 6

Tibet

As I watched Beijing come into view through the plane window, my first thought was, "I'm actually here, on my way to the assignment of a lifetime, working with professionals on a documentary about the people and the way of life of Tibet"

While rafting the Futaleufú, a premier whitewater river in Chile with Earth River, the expedition company producing the documentary, I'd caught the attention of one of the leaders. Seems a head of white hair counted for something, I was dubbed a "wisdom keeper" and would be called on to interview and record not only the native herdsman and villagers, but also the monks in the numerous monasteries along the way.

Having rafted the Upper Yangtze a year earlier, I jumped at the chance to run the "Wild Yak" (the Tibetan's name for the river) again. Because nothing I could have read, no stories I could have heard and no movie or video I could have seen, would have prepared me for the impact the Upper Yangtze and Tibet had on my very being.

Our entourage was made up of the producer, a cameraman, an actor for the action shots on the class four and five rapids we'd run, and our interpreter, a beautiful accomplished Tibetan girl of nineteen, a student at U of Xinxiang. We would meet two boatmen, a couple of native guides, and the truck driver when we reached Xining.

We were scheduled to do a preliminary run of the river with a commercial group of clients. This would afford us a chance to scope out the story line, the land, and the villagers, herdsmen, and monks that we'd be interacting with.

As we left the plane in Beijing, several uniformed officers approached the cameraman and politely confiscated his camera, explaining it would be returned to him when he left. It was a serious blow to the project, for it was that camera we had depended on to shoot the film in professional, high quality resolution. This loss scuttled the grand overall plan of the documentary, and though more than a bit dismayed, we soldiered on, determined to make the best of a bad deal, with the cameras the police had ignored. (Now, years later, the documentary films capturing the magnificence of Tibet and its people, rest somewhere in a box or drawer, perhaps a file cabinet. The end result of the smaller cameras just couldn't make the grade.)

After overnighting in Beijing we flew on to Xining, a city of over two million located on the Tibetan Plateau. Our trip to our put-in on the river was still three days away,

when we boarded a bus the next morning to carry us to the
Upper Yangtze.

Those three days of travel took us over mountain passes, in
view of snow-covered peaks reaching 12,000-15,000 feet
toward the heavens, then onto the plateau rimmed by low
rolling hills, a vast grassy plain that stretched as far as our
eyes could see. We came upon families of yak herdsmen
who follow the green grasses of summer with their animals.

Here and there on the hillsides sheep with their curly
white fleece grazed beside yaks. The yaks were impressive-
-huge animals (some weigh as much as 1,000 pounds) with
coats of long, coarse, jet black hair that hung beneath their
bellies. Some had white faces, some had long horns curving
forward. Nearby were clusters of canvas tents and an
occasional yurt belonging to the herders and their families.
Yak skin ropes strung beside them, held laundry, others
held colorful, tattered, silk prayer flags fluttering in the soft
breezes. It was August and the air was warm.

At the sight of those prayer flags, I remembered the prayers I had offered a year before, prayers to the God of Creation to help save 2,500 acres of beautiful waterfalls and forests in North Carolina from development. Some were whispered into prayer flags, another was thrown to the wind.

While doing extensive research about Tibet, prior to my trip the previous year, I'd read of the practice used by Tibetans to send prayers to their gods. And so I made my preparations. Before I left my Cedar Mountain home I had composed a prayer asking that those North Carolina lands be preserved, wrote it out, folded it carefully and packed it with my gear.

It was a hard climb to a monastery, high on a cliff above the river where I planned to offer my prayer, but a step at a time I got there. Given a warm welcome by the smiling monks, I reached into my backpack and pulled out the prayer. After the interpreter explained my mission to the monks, there was understanding in their eyes and smiles across their faces. As they nodded their heads and began chanting, I tore the prayer into small pieces. Tossing them into the air I watched as an updraft from the river carried them away. I like to think that somewhere the God of Creation heard or took notice of it, for the lands and waterfalls of the proposed development in North Carolina were acquired by the state and became DuPont State Forest a short month later. Prayers answered!

I shared the story with the crew as we drove on through small outpost villages of concrete block and corrugated metal, a few stores strung along the road selling basic supplies from the outside world. We overnighted in primitive guesthouses along the way, and leaned that yak dung burned in a small stove can heat a room as quickly as wood. Everywhere we were treated like honored guests by the townspeople, for very few westerners traveled these rugged paths.

Arriving at our put-in, we were met by uniformed officials who examined our credentials, then like kids with new toys, they sat in our boats, took the oars in their hands and maybe, in their imagination, left that beach and were on their way to the mouth of the Yangtze in the South China Sea, nearly 4,000 miles away.

And then we were off, to drift silently along this section of the upper Yangtze, lovingly referred to as the "River of Golden Sand" by Tibetans. Our lunch stops provided us with the chance to explore the sometimes sandy, sometimes rocky beaches and the fields beyond them. On a memorable day, after hiking a short distance, we came upon a field of dark blue larkspur in bloom, not just a few, but hundreds of spires of the plants, some more than three feet tall. The cameras rolled, and rolled again when we came upon blue poppy plants in another field, later in the day. Unforgettable seas of blue there in the highlands

Further downstream the river's name changed again, now it was the "River to Heaven." It took us by rushing tributaries, through deep granite canyons, past handsome *Mani* stones with *mantras*, or Tibetan prayers, carved on them. Coming out of a bend on the river, I noticed a number of eagles circling high above a cliff. Questioning the sight, I was told they were part of a sky burial, a funeral practice in which the bodies of the dead are placed on a mountain top to be picked clean by the eagles, or to just decompose.

Arriving back in Xining, we said good-bye to the commercial clients we had traveled with, and began the journey overland back up the river. Traveling in two Toyota Land Cruisers and a big, lumbering supply truck filled with our gear, motor breakdowns became the order of the day. When one quit, we all stopped while the hood of the machine was opened and the problems, both hidden and obvious were addressed. I learned early on to have my hiking boots on, ready to explore, or a good book at hand to pass the time away until the "let's go" was shouted.

At one stop I watched the Interpreter leave the group and walk back along the road we had traveled on. After ten minutes or so, I decided to walk after her, cause we usually stayed in a group and she was gone longer than I thought realistic for a private moment (which we all need and don't have to explain.)

Back around a couple curves on that dusty road, I came upon her kneeling down, placing the final rocks on a cairn she had built. It took me a moment or two to take in the scene and then it dawned on me-she had gone back to where we had noticed a dead rabbit on the roadway, had scooped out a grave for it, and had given the body a final resting place away from the indignities of this mechanized world that killed and continued to mangle.

I remembered lines Barry Lopez wrote in his book *Apologia* about carrying for burial what was left of the life and energy now stretched across the highway. "The raccoons and later, the red fox carry like sacks of wet gravel and sand. Each animal is like a solitary child's shoe in the road."

Once a man asked him, "Why do you bother?" "You never know," he replied. "The ones you give some semblance of burial, to whom you offer an apology, may have been like seers in a parallel culture. It is an act of respect, a technique of awareness."

Now, so far from home, it was a touching scene, that girl child of another culture, recognizing with reverence a life that had burned in a simple creature.

Returning to the river, we began the final phase of our trip. And our cameras rolled, capturing the majesty of the canyons, the stone villages tucked away in the hills, the villagers and their everyday life.

Approaching a settlement nestled high in the cliffs, I noticed a large number of young trees on the hillside, obviously a re-forestation project. It touched my conservationist heart, and I wondered who might have initiated the effort.

I had my chance to ask later in the day as I interviewed an older woman, a venerated elder of the village. We sat on a stone bench in the village center, sipping cups of Tibetan tea, a dark, strong blend fortified with a generous spoonful of yak butter.

During the interview I asked her about the trees on the hill, "why were they planted?" I expected an answer like "to prevent erosion" or "to keep the mountainside from slipping into the river." She looked at me. The interpreter

smiled as she translated her answer, "So we could sit in their shade." Then she added, "And sometimes we take food and eat there." I laughed and said, "So do my people, we call it a picnic."

It was an "*aha*" moment. Suddenly we connected on a little thing that bound us together. We shared an afternoon of stories and smiles, finding common bonds in picnics, families, puppies, and the beauty of sunsets.

The humanness that binds the family of man together.

After several days in that vast wilderness, we began to see more glimpses of civilization. Herdsman high in the hills tending their yaks, an occasional native walking along the shore, smoke rising from a fire in a village beyond our eyesight.

Our welcome at the monasteries we visited was heartwarming, as few foreign visitors make their way to those sacred temples. The monks would gather around to learn more about us, our trip and our world. And then invite us in to share theirs.

Walking through the massive carved doors of a temple, we were assaulted by the beauty inside. A page in the Lonely Planet Guide to Tibet had advised us that "Behind the whitewashed walls of every Tibetan Buddhist monastery lurks a hidden world of golden sculptures and rainbow-colored murals. These radiant artworks were clearly not inspired by the grey and ochre color scheme of the Himalayan landscape; Tibetan Buddhist art is, at its purest level, art of the imagination."

We entered a cavernous room with beautifully painted walls, beams, arches and altars, a golden statue of the Buddha, soft, colorful wall hangings, and prayer rugs of rich shades and tones. Taking a seat on a rug, we watched monks scurry about lighting incense and candles, while others, sitting cross legged on the floor chanted their prayers. As the perfume of the incense, the low murmur of chants and the deep vibrations of singing bowls reached me, I experienced a sacred moment in time: one that is inexplicable, one that will stay with me forever.

Near the end of our trip, around the campfires at night, talk among the guides often turned to the town of Yushu

and the excitement, magic, and treasures, we'd find there.
After long days of paddling, drifting, shooting rapids,
skirting rapids, putting up and taking down camp each day,
the town began to take on a fairy tale dimension.

On the day we arrived there, I found the magic and
excitement promised in that outpost town. Turkic, Han
Chinese, Tibetans, Uyghurs, monks, herders, craftsmen,
a veritable melting pot. Capturing the town square's very
center was a statue of a horse and rider, powerful muscles
of the horse straining as it reared skyward, the riders arm
was raised high in salute or victory. . . maybe defiance?
Colorful rainbows of banners flew across streets that were
filled with nomadic pastoralists, farmers, traders, and
townspeople mingling in their everyday business. It was a
busy scene, bicycles with little carts full of goods for the
market place inched along, an old chug-chugging-tractor,
the kind that saw light in the wheat fields of Wisconsin in
the 1920's with smoke puffing out of little, short, smoke
stacks, crawled by pulling flat beds of grain. A donkey,
decked out in harness with bright red plumes atop its
head, and a tinkling bell around its neck, plodded along
with goods piled high atop his back. Suddenly I
remembered the donkeys and the salt train I'd met on my
trek in Nepal, and wondered if this donkey would know
the thrill of an adventure like that. Or maybe it had.

I remember threading my way along streets and
through bazars, and being assaulted by the color and
richness of the scene. The handsome peoples of Turkic
and Han lineage, with strong high cheekbones, piercing
brown eyes and shiny black hair, reminded me of our
Native Americans. And well they might, for it was their

ancestors who crossed the Bering Strait thousands of years ago, to make a home in the Americas.

Some of the men wore a headpiece made of strands of red yarn twisted together to form a thick crown, which they carried regally. Another had a faded blue cowboy hat perched atop his head, while others wore old fedoras and kept warm in simple, high collared jackets, made popular during Mao Zedong's regime. The tribesmen from the highlands looked quite dashing and commanded attention as they strolled along in their long, dark, yak skin robes and boots, as smiling monks scurried along clothed in burgundy robes, their heads shaven, eyes twinkling.

Lining the streets were stalls filled with low tables that held canvas and burlap bags displaying contents of grains, dried food, spices, and medicinal herbs. Here and there were tables piled high with Incredible chunks of uncut turquoise, beside them lay handsome turquoise and coral necklaces, rings, amulets, and hair pieces, prized and worn by both men and women.

I came upon a small, hand fashioned wood and bamboo pail filled with yak butter. There was utter disbelief among the nomads, when my interpreter and I tried to explain that I wanted just the pail without the butter. The merchant was incredulous, but finally shrugged, removed the butter and handed it to me. It remains a treasured memento on my library table, filled with seasonal flowers.

Then, strolling past a tent with its street side showcase full of ancient, ink stained, hand-carved woodblocks, I found the treasure I had hoped to find. On the wall behind the blocks hung *thangkas*, paintings or embroideries of Tibetan silk, royal blue, deep green, crimson red, and gold. Finding one of these tapestries made of embroidery, usually depicting a Buddhist deity, famous scene, or mandala of some sort in a true Tibetan market, was something I had dreamed of. With a smile and the Tibetan greeting, "*Tasha deli*" I began the bargaining game.

It was, simply put, an incredible journey....... to have entree to that fabled land, to walk through the villages and nomad camps and mingle with the people, to experience the holy and magical moments in the monasteries, to simply revel in the beauty and vastness of the land around me was an experience, and a privilege that must rank among the greatest a traveler could wish for.

Epilogue

I'd learned early on the joy of traveling alone, immersing myself in another culture and living as they did; In a yurt, ger, tepee, igloo, or in primitive inns and guest houses, sleeping where they slept, eating what they ate, traveling with them on their paths, and finding joy in the things that made them smile.

The rewards of being alone, without the comfort or crutch of a traveling companion, taught me to rely on strangers for protection, understanding, and companionship. It also afforded me a wealth of memorable moments and experiences.

While never being without a guide who had at least a rudimentary grasp of English, having to be understood through gestures, the unspoken language of eyes and facial expression, took the skills of communication to a new level. Challenging and at times frustrating, but always rewarding when an "aha" moment occurred, that sudden moment when the light of understanding shone in our eyes.

Acknowledgement

I begin by offering heartfelt gratitude to my children, Jacquelyn and William. Thanks for believing in me, for supporting and encouraging me to take those journeys; to travel on, to find my voice.

Thanks to the Tampa physician and physical therapists, who helped me achieve the maximal use of my middle-aged muscles and limbs. Without their help, I'd never have known the joy of "keepin' on, walkin' on."

Thanks to the Wordsmiths, the writing group formed under the direction of Nancy Purcell, who, along with Rich Schram and Bud Shepard, have followed my peregrinations over the years, correcting and encouraging me.

To Attracta Hutchinson, Joe Hall, Betsy Craig, Sara Baird, Ann Ives, Alexandra Burrowghs, Janet Benway, Judy Pierce, Laura Knight, Fred Cohn, Ben Rankin, Cheryl Groeneveld, Susan Gabriel, Susan Zelle, and Kathy Evernham, who at one time were all members of that august group, helping me with their questions, comments, and criticisms,

To Star Swanson, another Wordsmith who offered her scholarly talents to help me polish the adventures.

To Elizabeth Jennings, whose thoughtful advise about story content helped me format this book.

To Sandy Perry for locating information about my long ago teacher.

To Kris Blair for her help in probing the mysteries of Machu Picchu.

To Gus Napier, whose photographic talents helped breathe life into a tired photo.

To Editor Wayne Drumheller who patiently walked me through the page formatting and publishing process.

To Helen Adams, my Computer Guru, who helped me unravel the mystery of sending my story as a "Word Doc."

To Vicki Lane for her editorial help, and above all, for her sage advice.

And lastly, heartfelt thanks to my friend and mentor, the late Allene "Linky" Stone, for her counsel given to me many years ago: "If you can conceive it, you can achieve it."

I did, "Linky." And now I have.

Photographs

P.   7 Mountain Terrace View
P. 17 Aleen at Elephant Compound
P. 41 Pakistan Guard
P. 43 Ironing Sheets
P. 47 Young Kalash Girl
P. 60 Friends Dressed to Cross Glacier
P. 65 Siberian Brown Bear
P. 71 New Friends and Bucket of Blueberries
P. 73 Nunavut Day, April 1, 1999
P. 83 Nunavut Flag
P. 92 Dog Sledding in Artic
P. 93 High Above the River
P. 95 Tibetan Herdsman
P. 96 Tossing a Prayer to the Gods
P. 100 Village Elder
All photographs courtesy of the author

About the Author

Aleen grew up in a small town in Wisconsin, and was encouraged to explore the fields and hills around her home town as a young girl. She was fortunate to be raised by parents who placed a strong value on time spent out of doors. She learned to respect the natural world and people of all races and faiths at an early age.

She attended the University of Wisconsin before marriage. Her attention and volunteer efforts turned to environmental activism after reading Rachel Carson's *Silent Spring*. She subsequently helped lead the fight to save both the Green Swamp in Florida and DuPont State Recreational Forest in North Carolina from incompatible development. Aleen currently serves on environmental and philanthropic boards in both Florida and North Carolina.

An adventure traveler, she has rafted rivers and climbed mountains on six continents. Living and traveling with indigenous people, she sought and found the humanness, that binds the family of man together.

Keepin' On, Walkin' On

Made in the USA
Columbia, SC
03 August 2018